From the Classroom to Congress,
A Memoir

Melissa May

Dedication

This book is dedicated to the resilient communities of the Inland Empire, particularly those who have borne the brunt of environmental injustice for far too long. Your strength, your unwavering spirit, and your tireless advocacy in the face of adversity have been an inspiration. This work is a testament to your collective struggle and a commitment to amplifying your voices on the national stage. It is also dedicated to the memory of those whose lives have been tragically cut short or irrevocably altered by environmental hazards – a stark reminder of the urgent need for change.

To my family, whose unwavering support and understanding have been the bedrock of my journey, thank you for your love and patience. To my mentors and colleagues, whose guidance and collaboration have been invaluable, your dedication and belief in the power of collective action have had a profoundly positive impact on my life and work. Finally, this book is dedicated to the next generation – the young people who will inherit the planet we leave behind. May this story serve as a beacon of hope, a reminder that even in the face of seemingly insurmountable challenges, positive change is possible. May it ignite within them a fierce determination to build a more just and sustainable future for all.

May they never forget that their voices matter, that their actions have consequences, and that they possess the power to shape a healthier, more equitable world.

TABLE OF CONTENTS

Preface

I was not born into comfort or certainty—I was born into the fight. Every story in these pages rises out of the smog-filled valleys and vibrant neighborhoods of the Inland Empire, where hope runs headlong into injustice and community is forged in adversity.

This memoir is not just a recounting of my journey from crowded classrooms to the weight of Congress. It's a testament to resilience: the stubborn will of a mother at a kitchen table, the courage of neighbors organizing beneath flickering lights, the defiance of children who refuse to let the world define their worth.

I don't write these words as a victory lap, but as a map of scars and triumphs—a record of the moments that shaped me, the setbacks that honed my resolve, and the collective strength that made progress possible. Through stories of polluted air and unyielding activism, I want you to see the people too often left behind, to feel the pulse of a movement rising from everyday acts of defiance.

This book is for anyone who's ever wondered if their voice can matter. My hope is that by sharing these truths—the raw, difficult, unvarnished reality and the hope that survives it—you will find something of your own power. Justice has never been handed down; it's built from the ground up, by those who refuse to wait for permission.

This isn't just my story. It's the story of a community that taught me to fight for a world where every breath is a promise of possibility, not a gamble with fate. I invite you to take the next step with us. The struggle continues—one breath, one act, one story at a time.

Introduction

From Classroom to Congress is more than just a title; it encapsulates the core of my life's journey. It's a narrative that begins in the smog-choked streets of the Inland Empire, a region often overlooked yet burdened by some of the nation's worst environmental injustices. Growing up amidst this reality shaped my worldview, igniting a passion for environmental justice that would guide my career as an educator, activist, and ultimately, a politician. This book is not a linear progression; it's a tapestry woven from personal experiences, investigative reporting, and political engagement.

It explores the complexities of environmental racism, highlighting how marginalized communities disproportionately bear the burden of pollution and environmental degradation. It delves into the challenges faced by grassroots movements, examining the strategies employed to build coalitions, mobilize communities, and challenge entrenched power structures. It examines the role of digital media in amplifying marginalized voices and accelerating the pace of social change, demonstrating how technology can be leveraged to create impactful narratives that transcend geographical limitations.

The book also examines the crucial intersection of environmental justice and other critical social issues – namely, inadequate housing, systemic poverty, and educational inequities. It illustrates how these interconnected issues contribute to a vicious cycle of environmental degradation and social injustice, highlighting the need for holistic, multifaceted approaches to achieve sustainable and equitable solutions. Through personal anecdotes and meticulously researched data, the book illustrates the vital importance of community-led solutions and the remarkable resilience of the people fighting for a better tomorrow.

This journey is far from over; the fight for environmental justice continues. My hope is that this book will not only inform, but also inspire readers to become active participants in this crucial movement.

Chapter 1:

Roots in the Inland Empire

I was born to fight. In the way some people are born to sing, or paint, or write. My life—every breath, every battle—was preparing me to become the woman who would one day stand on the campaign trail and declare, "I come from a place no one wants to see and the air feels like sandpaper."

I grew up in Ontario, California. The Inland Empire—a sprawling region east of Los Angeles, etched not just by the San Gabriel and San Bernardino mountains, but also by a pervasive, almost invisible enemy: pollution. Not the polished coastal California people imagine, but the dry, smog-filled corridor where poverty and pollution coexisted as naturally as the tumbleweeds that rolled across our streets.

My childhood memories are interwoven with the acrid tang of smog, a constant haze that draped itself over our community, blurring the sharp lines of the mountains and casting a pall over everything. My earliest memories are stitched with the smell of diesel and the sound of sirens. It wasn't a picturesque backdrop; it was a persistent threat, a silent assault on our health and well-being.

Our neighborhood, nestled amongst sprawling industrial parks and busy freeways, was far from idyllic. Trucks thundered past our schools, delivering goods that fed the wealth of cities we would never touch. The air was thick with the stench of refineries and factories, a cocktail of noxious fumes that burned in our throats and stung our eyes. Days were often marked by a hazy sun, its light muted by the persistent layer of smog, and the nights were filled with the low hum of industrial machinery, a relentless soundtrack to our lives. The air itself felt heavy, laden with pollutants, an invisible weight that pressed down on us all.

In the neighborhoods I called home, asthma inhalers were as common as backpacks, and playgrounds were framed by chain-link fences. This wasn't unusual. In our community, kids carried inhalers like other children carried lunch money. Asthma was as common as Spanish on our tongues, as inevitable as the freight trains that rumbled past our house at all hours, carrying chemicals to and from the industrial plants that ringed our world.

The most readily visible evidence of pollution was the smog itself. Thick brown clouds would often descend, obscuring the sun and turning the sky into a murky canvas of orange and grey. This was not simply an inconvenience; it was a constant reminder of the unhealthy environment in which we lived. Visibility was often severely reduced, creating driving hazards and a sense of claustrophobia that permeated our daily lives. Children played in this polluted air, breathing it in with every gasp, their lungs silently absorbing the toxins that would later manifest in various health problems.

Our water wasn't spared either. Stories of contaminated water sources were commonplace within our community, whispers passed from one neighbor to another like clandestine secrets. We were told stories of wells contaminated by industrial runoff, the water tainted with heavy metals and other hazardous materials. There were instances of discolored water coming from our taps, creating apprehension and fear within our households. While the visible signs weren't always immediately apparent, there was an undeniable anxiety connected to the very water we drank and used daily. Fear was ingrained in us early on; a deep-seated worry about the long-term effects of the invisible dangers that surrounded us.

The consequences of this pervasive pollution were undeniably felt within our community. Respiratory illnesses, particularly asthma, were rampant amongst children, like a common cold spread throughout the neighborhood. My family wasn't immune. I vividly remember countless nights spent coughing, my lungs burning, while the familiar aroma of menthol from vapor rubs filled the air. I remember my brother struggling for breath, his face contorted in silent pain, another victim of this environmental injustice. Many in our community faced similar struggles, a shared burden imposed by the neglectful systems that failed to protect us.

These were not isolated incidents; the impact of pollution on the health of our community extended far beyond individual cases. This isn't just pollution; it's a silent plague, a toxic shroud blanketing communities where up to one in five children gasp for air, their tiny chests heaving with the weight of asthma. Imagine the fear in a mother's eyes as she watches her child's face contort in a coughing fit, the desperate wheezing a constant soundtrack to their lives. The statistics – a horrifying 20% asthma rate in some areas – don't capture the raw terror, the constant anxiety, the pervasive dread that settles like smog on the soul. This isn't a ranking; it's a condemnation. It's a death sentence, meted out slowly, invisibly, one gasping breath at a time.

The data revealed a harsh reality of environmental injustice— one that weighed heaviest on low-income communities and communities of color like ours. Our neighborhood stood as a living testament to the devastating toll of unchecked industrial pollution and the systemic failures that allowed it to thrive. It was a constant, painful reminder of the deep-rooted inequities woven into the fabric of our society.

The statistics spoke volumes, underscoring the undeniable link between environmental pollution and health disparities. Asthma and other respiratory illnesses plagued our zip code at rates far above the national average—a cold, indisputable truth that echoed the daily struggles we witnessed around us. These numbers weren't just data points; they were our neighbors, our friends, our families—facing the silent, invisible burdens of toxic air.

It wasn't a coincidence—it was the legacy of decades of systemic neglect, a pattern of prioritizing profit over people.

But the impact extended beyond our health. Pollution casts a long, suffocating shadow over our everyday lives. The ever-present smog dimmed our skies and limited our freedom to play, breathe, or simply exist outdoors. Parks lost their magic, walks lost their ease, and joy often came with a gasp for air. Our vibrant world faded beneath a persistent grey haze, muting the color, wonder, and possibility of our environment. The heavy air pushed us indoors, into spaces that felt safer but no less confining. We exchanged open skies for closed windows—a trade that felt deeply unjust and profoundly isolating.

The prospect of a future defined by clean air, healthy landscapes, and abundant opportunities seemed distant, almost unattainable —a fantasy that contrasted sharply with the grim reality of our everyday lives. We knew, even at a young age, that this was not a normal way to live, and that something needed to change. This awareness, this growing understanding of environmental injustice, was the first seed of activism that would eventually blossom into a lifelong commitment to change. The very air we breathed fueled the fire within me, a fire that continues to burn brightly today.

The pervasive nature of pollution wasn't only about the physical consequences but also the psychological impact. There was an ever-present awareness of the unseen dangers, a subtle anxiety that shaped our daily lives. The fear that our children would suffer the same health problems, that the damage to our bodies was irreversible, weighed heavily on us.

This wasn't just about poor air quality; it was about the fear of an uncertain future, a future burdened by the legacy of environmental neglect. The psychological toll was significant, a pervasive sense of helplessness that hung in the air, as thick and suffocating as the smog itself.

The pollution wasn't simply a backdrop; it was an integral part of our community's story, a defining characteristic of our existence. It permeated every aspect of our lives, from the air we breathed to the water we drank, to our shared concerns about our children's health and job opportunities. It was a shared struggle, a collective experience that bound us together, forging a strong sense of community. This collective trauma, this shared experience of environmental injustice, would be the foundation for the activism that would define a community's future.

Growing up surrounded by this pollution wasn't merely a childhood experience; it was a foundational element of my identity, shaping my worldview and fueling my passion for environmental justice. It was the crucible in which my activism was forged, the catalyst that propelled me from the classroom to the Congressional campaign trail, on a mission to fight for the health and well-being of communities facing similar battles against environmental injustice. It is a story of the power of personal experiences to inspire transformative change and a legacy that compels me to continue the fight for a healthier and more just future for all. The smog of my childhood and the lack of job opportunities, once an unwelcome constant, became the driving force behind my life's work, a reminder of the urgent need for environmental and social justice and the strength that can be found in the collective voices of a community united in their fight for a better world.

My early education in the Inland Empire was a paradoxical experience. While the curriculum celebrated the wonders of the natural world—life cycles of plants, majestic mountains, and the delicate balance of ecosystems—the reality outside our classroom windows painted a starkly different picture. We studied photosynthesis in science class, yet the smog often obscured the sun, hindering the very process we were learning about.

Textbooks described pristine forests and clear rivers, but our community's air and water were consistently compromised. This dissonance between the idealized world in our lessons and the harsh realities of our environment created a profound cognitive tension that shaped my worldview.

My teachers were dedicated and hardworking, many of whom were residents of the Inland Empire and understood the environmental challenges we faced. Yet, the resources to address these issues within the curriculum were limited. Environmental education was often reduced to a single unit in science class, failing to capture the depth and urgency of the injustices surrounding us. Discussions about pollution were brief and abstract, rarely connected to our lived experiences. Textbooks, while informative, lacked the immediacy and gravity that matched the threats we faced daily. This disconnect fostered a growing frustration and a sense that something was deeply wrong—an awareness that extended far beyond the typical anxieties of childhood.

One field trip remains etched in my memory. We visited a local park, intended as a sanctuary of nature amidst the urban sprawl. Instead, the air quality was poor, the smog casting a gray pall over everything. The vibrant colors of plants and flowers were muted, and the air reeked of industrial emissions. During our hike, a classmate suffered a severe asthma attack, a stark reminder that pollution wasn't just an abstract concept—it was a direct threat to our health. That student, beloved by many, later passed away. This moment transformed my vague unease into a visceral understanding of environmental injustice, shifting my perspective from academic comprehension to lived reality.

The lack of robust environmental education left a void that my classmates and I filled with our own observations. We noticed the air quality index fluctuating wildly, and the correlation between smoggy days and increased illnesses. We saw discolored waterways and dead fish floating on the surface, silent evidence of contamination. We overheard adults whispering about polluted water sources and rising respiratory illnesses. This informal, lived education was more impactful than any lesson plan, forging an indelible link between the environment and social justice.

My own health struggles reinforced this connection. Frequent respiratory infections, bronchitis, and persistent coughs were common among my peers and me. Medical professionals often dismissed these ailments as allergies or colds, ignoring the obvious link to our polluted environment. This dismissal deepened the sense that our concerns were being overlooked, further galvanizing my desire for systemic change in education and healthcare.

The health challenges extended beyond individuals to entire families. Parents worried about their children's well-being, while many struggled to afford medical care. These struggles, rooted in environmental neglect, weren't just personal observations—they were a collective call to action. They ignited a desire within me to fight for a future where environmental justice was not an abstract ideal but a lived reality.

Pollution also shaped our social lives. Outdoor activities, a cornerstone of childhood, were often curtailed by smog. The heavy air confined us indoors, limiting our ability to play, explore, and connect with nature. This shared experience of environmental inequality created a sense of community, binding us together in a common struggle.

The inequities were glaring. Low-income communities and communities of color bore the brunt of pollution, a pattern of environmental racism that became central to my later work. These disparities weren't random; they were the result of systemic injustices—policies prioritizing profit over people and regulatory failures to protect vulnerable communities.

This realization was pivotal, highlighting the need for accountability, enforcement, and funding to create meaningful change.

This awakening wasn't a single moment of epiphany but a culmination of interconnected experiences: the gap between classroom teachings and real-world observations, personal health struggles, and the shared challenges of my community. It was the slow accumulation of evidence that shaped my understanding of environmental injustice. This wasn't just about pollution; it was about systemic inequalities and the disproportionate burden placed on marginalized communities without the resources or political power to protect themselves. The smog-choked skies of my childhood, once a source of frustration and ill health, became the fuel for a lifelong mission to challenge power structures and advocate for a healthier, more equitable world.

These experiences were part of a larger narrative of environmental injustice in the Inland Empire. The disparity in environmental burdens between affluent and low-income neighborhoods, between predominantly white communities and communities of color, was undeniable. This early awareness instilled in me a profound sense of responsibility and a conviction to fight for a just and equitable future. The seeds of activism were sown early, nurtured by the harsh realities of my surroundings, and blossomed into a career dedicated to environmental justice.

Ironically, the lack of comprehensive environmental education became a powerful catalyst for my learning and activism. It exposed the gaps in our understanding and underscored the urgency for systemic change. The silence on these critical issues within formal education forced us to seek answers elsewhere, transforming us into self-educated activists driven by personal experiences and community concerns. This demonstrated the power of lived experiences to fuel grassroots movements for change.

My early education and awakening were not just about absorbing facts but about understanding the intricate relationship between environment and social justice. The injustices I witnessed were manifestations of larger systemic issues, connecting local challenges to global patterns of environmental degradation and inequality. This understanding fueled my desire to advocate for marginalized communities and fight for equity, fairness, and well-being for all. These formative years laid the foundation for a life dedicated to environmental justice, built not just on academic learning but on the visceral experiences of a childhood marked by pollution. They solidified my belief that true change requires addressing root causes, dismantling environmental racism, and creating a healthier, more equitable world.

The Inland Empire, with its sprawling landscape and vibrant mix of cultures, was more than just a geographical location—it was a crucible where community resilience and social justice were forged. My family, deeply rooted in Mexican heritage, instilled in me the importance of familia, collective responsibility, and an unwavering belief in the power of la comunidad. These values weren't abstract ideals; they were lived realities, demonstrated daily in the way our community rallied around those in need, shared resources, and navigated life's challenges together.

Our local church, a vibrant hub of community life, further reinforced these values. It wasn't just a place of worship; it was a center of support and a catalyst for action. Through food drives, clothing donations, and fundraising initiatives, I learned the power of collective responsibility and the profound impact of even small acts of kindness. These experiences taught me empathy, the importance of contributing to the well-being of others, and the transformative potential of community action.

Beyond my family and the church, the larger community played a pivotal role in shaping my worldview. I witnessed the strength and resilience of our neighbors as they faced adversity, supporting one another during hardships and organizing to address shared concerns. This wasn't a passive observation—I actively participated in these efforts, experiencing firsthand the tangible impact of collective action.

One particularly formative experience was our neighborhood's fight to improve local parks. Despite their importance as community spaces, the parks were neglected, with broken equipment, overgrown vegetation, and poor maintenance. Refusing to accept this, neighbors organized meetings, drafted proposals, and worked with local officials to secure funding for renovations. The transformation of these parks into safe, vibrant spaces for recreation and connection was a powerful lesson in the effectiveness of community organizing and the potential for collective action to create meaningful change.

My involvement in the local youth center further deepened my understanding of community and social responsibility. The center, a haven for young people, provided a safe space for recreation, education, and connection. Its dedicated staff fostered leadership, collaboration, and a sense of purpose in us. Through various programs, I developed leadership skills and learned the value of teamwork in achieving shared goals.

At the same time, I became acutely aware of the pervasive inequalities in our community—disparities in access to resources and opportunities that were often tied to socioeconomic status and ethnicity. The youth center also exposed me to the broader challenges our community faced. I saw families grappling with poverty, unemployment, and limited access to basic necessities like healthcare and education. These experiences underscored the urgency of addressing systemic inequalities and the critical role of collective action in building a more just society.

The lessons I gained through the church, community organizations, and youth programs were far more than extracurricular activities—they were foundational lessons in citizenship, leadership, and social responsibility. They provided an invaluable education in community organizing and the power of collective action to address social and environmental injustices. These experiences instilled in me a deep belief in the ability of communities to effect positive change and fueled my desire to make a meaningful difference.

The community's response to environmental challenges offered further lessons in resilience and action. Air pollution, contaminated water, and neglected public spaces were not passively accepted. Instead, the community mobilized—organizing protests, advocacy campaigns, and lobbying efforts to demand improvements in air and water quality, infrastructure, and environmental protections.

While these efforts often faced bureaucratic obstacles and resistance from powerful interests, the small victories we achieved reinforced the belief that persistence and collaboration could lead to real change. Participating in these initiatives was both challenging and rewarding. I learned the importance of strategic planning, the value of persistence, and the frustration of navigating systemic barriers. Yet, the successes, however incremental, were deeply satisfying and affirmed the power of collective action.

Community wasn't just about organizing; it was also about mutual support and shared experiences. During crises—whether natural disasters or personal tragedies—the community came together, offering comfort, assistance, and solidarity. This collective empathy created a strong social fabric, fostering resilience and a profound sense of belonging.

This sense of community wasn't merely about proximity; it was a shared identity forged through collective experiences and a common commitment to addressing challenges. It was a network of relationships and mutual support that shaped my understanding of social responsibility and fueled my commitment to environmental justice.

This interconnectedness fostered a strong sense of collective efficacy—the belief that together, we could make a difference. This belief wasn't theoretical; it was demonstrated time and again in our community's ability to organize, mobilize, and achieve meaningful change despite limited resources. This shared conviction became the foundation for my later efforts to mobilize broader movements for environmental justice. It required all of us to believe in one another and to recognize our shared bond, even across differing political affiliations, to accomplish meaningful progress.

The community also provided a rich environment for learning that extended far beyond formal education. The lessons I gained through direct participation in community initiatives and observing the actions of others were as valuable—if not more so— than anything I learned in a classroom. This experiential learning fostered critical thinking, problem-solving skills, and a deep sense of social responsibility.

The understanding I gained in the Inland Empire wasn't just a collection of facts; it was a lived experience, an immersion in the complexities of community life—its struggles, triumphs, and enduring power to effect change. These experiences formed the bedrock of my activism, shaping my beliefs, informing my strategies, and driving my commitment to building a more just and equitable world. The community wasn't just a backdrop; it was the foundation upon which my dedication to environmental justice was conceived, nurtured, and ultimately launched.

The stirrings of activism within me weren't born of a single epiphany but rather a gradual awakening—a slow burn fueled by the accumulation of small injustices that, when viewed collectively, revealed a stark picture of systemic failure. One such incident involved the proposed construction of a warehouse on the edge of our predominantly Latino neighborhood. Promising jobs and economic growth, the project was presented as a boon to our struggling community. However, the reality was far less promising:

the jobs offered did not provide livable wages, and the environmental risks posed by the warehouse were substantial.

Air quality in our region was already a pressing concern, worsened by existing industrial facilities and heavy truck traffic. The proposed warehouse, with its potential for increased emissions, felt like a direct threat to our health—especially to the elderly, children, and those with pre-existing respiratory conditions. Community meetings to discuss the project were fraught with tension. Developers, backed by influential politicians, delivered polished presentations touting economic benefits while downplaying the environmental and health consequences. Many community members, predominantly Spanish-speaking and unfamiliar with the complexities of Environmental Impact Reports (EIRs), found themselves overwhelmed and outmatched.

As the local government pushed forward with rezoning efforts to accommodate the warehouse, it became clear that the process was shrouded in complexity. Technical jargon and legalese created a barrier for those trying to understand the implications. The Environmental Impact Reports, intended to be comprehensive, appeared to be skewed in favor of the project, selectively presenting data to minimize perceived risks. At town hall meetings, I listened to the passionate pleas of my neighbors, who feared for the future of our community. Despite their assurances of mitigation measures, the developers' promises rang hollow. We knew the influx of heavy industry would pollute our air and endanger the very people they claimed to want to employ.

The developers' financial resources and political connections gave them a clear advantage, but our community persisted. We rallied, protested, and educated ourselves on the intricacies of the approval process, determined to expose discrepancies and hold those in power accountable. It was a daunting task, but our unity and resolve gave us strength as we fought to protect the heart and soul of our neighborhood.

This experience highlighted a glaring disparity in access to information and resources. The voices of our predominantly low-income, minority community were drowned out by the powerful interests of developers and their political allies. The promises of economic benefits felt hollow in the face of the tangible threats to our health and environment. While initially disheartening, this experience ignited a fire within me and my community. It was my first direct encounter with environmental injustice, where marginalized communities bore the brunt of environmental hazards while reaping few, if any, benefits.

The frustration I felt fueled a desire to understand the mechanisms that allowed such injustices to persist. I began researching environmental regulations, attending public hearings, and studying the impact of industrial pollution on vulnerable populations. What I uncovered was a pattern of systemic neglect: environmental regulations were often inadequately enforced in low-income communities and communities of color, perpetuating a profound disparity in environmental protection at the local level.

This systemic disregard was further underscored by the chronic underfunding of our local schools, which predominantly served Latino students. While wealthier neighboring districts boasted state-of-the-art facilities and ample resources, our schools struggled with outdated equipment, overcrowded classrooms, and a lack of essential materials. This inequitable distribution of resources wasn't just a matter of funding; it reflected deeper systemic biases that prioritized affluent communities over marginalized ones. The impact on our youth was profound, limiting their access to quality education and hindering their future opportunities.

The stark contrast between our struggling schools and the well-resourced neighboring districts served as a constant reminder of the systemic inequalities that shape our community. Volunteering at the local community center, I tutored students and witnessed firsthand the challenges they faced in overcoming these barriers. It was a sobering experience that deepened my commitment to addressing these inequities.

Another pivotal moment came with the contamination of our local water supply. A fireworks manufacturing site outside city limits leaked toxic chemicals into the groundwater, affecting several neighborhoods. The initial response from local officials was slow and inadequate, and it took intervention from the Supreme Court to designate the site as a Superfund location. This incident underscored the failures of local governance to protect its citizens and highlighted the vulnerability of our community to environmental hazards.

The long-term health risks were devastating, particularly for children and the elderly, and the lack of urgency from officials was a stark reminder of the systemic neglect we faced. Outraged, the community organized protests, demanded accountability, and lobbied for stronger environmental regulations. While the initial efforts were disorganized—hampered by language barriers and limited resources—the collective anger and determination fueled a sense of unity and purpose. This response revealed the power of our community to mobilize and demand justice, even in the face of significant obstacles.

My involvement in these efforts provided invaluable lessons in activism. I learned the intricacies of grassroots mobilization, the importance of strategic planning, and the need for persistent advocacy. The process was far from easy; we faced bureaucratic hurdles, opposition from powerful interests, and the constant challenge of securing resources. Yet, the small victories we achieved were deeply satisfying, reinforcing my belief in the transformative power of community organizing.

These experiences weren't isolated incidents but interconnected threads in a larger tapestry of injustice. The proposed warehouse, the underfunded schools, and the contaminated water supply were all symptoms of a deeper systemic problem: the disproportionate burden placed on marginalized communities to bear the costs of environmental degradation and social inequality. This realization solidified my decision to dedicate myself to activism—to become a voice for the voiceless and fight for a more just and equitable society.

This commitment wasn't made lightly; it was forged in the crucible of community struggle, fueled by experiences of injustice, and strengthened by the belief in the power of collective action. The seeds of activism were sown in the heart of the Inland Empire, nurtured by the resilience of our community, and blossomed into a lifelong dedication to social and environmental justice.

This commitment would later shape my work in education and politics, providing the framework for my efforts to create systemic change. I learned that the fight for justice is not a sprint but a marathon—requiring sustained effort, unwavering determination, and an unyielding commitment to the principles of diversity, equity, and inclusion.

The culmination of these experiences—the warehouses, the underfunded schools, the contaminated water—didn't just ignite a spark; they set my soul ablaze. The simmering frustration I had felt for years, a quiet hum of discontent at the inequities surrounding me, erupted into a roaring inferno. I could no longer stand idly by while the health and

well-being of my community, especially its most vulnerable members, were sacrificed at the altar of corporate greed and political apathy. This wasn't just about environmental justice; it was about social justice—the fundamental right to a safe and healthy life, free from the oppressive weight of systemic inequality.

As a science teacher, a role I had embraced with passion and dedication, I began to feel that my work, while meaningful, was insufficient in the face of the urgent need for systemic change. The lessons I taught in the classroom, however valuable, paled in comparison to the real-world lessons unfolding outside the school walls—lessons in power, privilege, and the persistent struggle for equity. My students, brimming with potential, were being constrained by the very systems designed to educate and empower them. How could I, in good conscience, teach science while ignoring the larger scientific and social realities shaping their lives?

The decision to transition from teaching to full-time activism wasn't a sudden leap but a gradual climb—a careful scaling of a steep and uncertain mountain. There were moments of doubt, of questioning my abilities and the impact of my efforts. Leaving a secure career path, one that provided stability and purpose, was daunting. The financial implications were significant, and the sacrifices loomed large. But the weight of injustice felt far heavier than any personal cost I might bear.

The support of my family and friends proved invaluable during this transition. My husband, steadfast and unwavering, provided both emotional and practical support, understanding the deep conviction driving my decision. My family, deeply rooted in the Inland Empire, recognized the urgency of the fight and embraced my commitment to justice. Their belief in me served as an anchor, giving me the strength to navigate the turbulent waters ahead.

Yet, the journey was not without its challenges. The lack of a steady income forced significant lifestyle adjustments. Long hours dedicated to activism, often at the expense of rest and personal time, took a toll on my physical and emotional well-being. The constant battles against powerful interests and entrenched systems left me drained and, at times, despondent. There were moments when the weight of responsibility felt almost unbearable, when the obstacles seemed insurmountable, threatening to extinguish the fire within me.

But the unwavering support of my community and the collective spirit of those fighting alongside me provided a wellspring of resilience. The shared determination to create a better future infused me with renewed purpose. Small but significant victories validated my decision to leave the classroom and dedicate myself fully to activism. One such victory came in the City of Ontario, where we successfully influenced redistricting efforts, ensuring fairer representation for marginalized communities. This win ignited a fire within me, proving that our efforts could make a tangible difference.

Buoyed by this success, we turned our attention to the local school board, where inequities in education had long been a pressing issue. Through tireless advocacy, we secured commitments to allocate more resources to underfunded schools and address systemic disparities that had hindered our children's education. The school board's decision to act was a testament to the power of our collective voice.

Another memorable triumph was preserving 70 acres of Prop 70-protected agricultural land from being sold to a warehouse developer. This land, a symbol of our community's rich farming heritage, was saved from the encroachment of industrialization. These victories, though modest in the grand scheme, fueled my passion and reinforced the belief that grassroots efforts could create meaningful change. Each incremental gain served as a reminder that collective action, no matter how challenging, could yield significant results.

A pivotal moment came during a community forum on environmental justice. After months of researching the Environmental Impact Report (EIR) for a proposed warehouse—deciphering dense regulatory documents, analyzing the city's general plan, and studying air pollution data from CalEnviro—I presented my findings to a diverse audience. Community members, civil rights organizations, law firms, media outlets, local officials, and even representatives from the development company were in attendance.

My presentation, driven by passion and backed by meticulous research, resonated deeply. People who had felt powerless and unheard were now empowered by the information I shared, energized by the possibility of challenging the status quo. It wasn't just a recitation of facts; it was a call to action, a rallying cry for collective engagement. The response was overwhelming. What began as an informational session transformed into a powerful demonstration of community solidarity, fueled by a shared commitment to environmental justice.

The success of the forum galvanized further efforts. Emboldened by their collective strength, community members organized protests, demanded greater transparency from local officials, and lobbied for stronger environmental regulations. The movement gained momentum, attracting media attention and bringing visibility to the issues we were fighting to address. Our collective action resulted in significant delays to the warehouse project, buying us precious time to organize and strategize further.

My role in the movement evolved beyond research and analysis. I became a liaison, connecting community groups, coordinating efforts, and strategizing actions. I learned the intricacies of community organizing, the importance of building alliances, and the power of strategic communication. I discovered how to harness storytelling to transform complex issues into relatable narratives that resonated across diverse audiences.

The transition from science teacher to community activist wasn't just a change in profession; it was a transformation of identity. It was a shedding of the familiar comfort of a predictable routine and an embrace of the unpredictable terrain of social justice activism. It was a recognition that true education extends far beyond the classroom, encompassing the broader social and environmental contexts that shape the lives of my students and my community.

This journey was marked by profound challenges and remarkable triumphs. The emotional toll was undeniable, but the sense of purpose and fulfillment far outweighed the difficulties. The sacrifices—financial instability, long hours, emotional exhaustion—paled in comparison to the impact of our work. The power of collective action, the realization that ordinary people united by a common cause can effect significant change, became a constant source of motivation. I learned that the fight for justice is not a sprint but a marathon, requiring persistence, resilience, and an unyielding belief in the power of people.

The lessons I learned during this pivotal phase of my life became invaluable in my subsequent work in education and politics. The experiences forged in the crucible of community activism shaped my approach to teaching and public service, imbuing my work with a profound sense of social responsibility and a deep commitment to uplifting marginalized communities. The roots of my activism, planted firmly in the soil of the Inland Empire, continued to nurture my lifelong dedication to social and environmental justice.

This was the turning point—from a teacher imparting knowledge within classroom walls to an activist fighting to change the world outside them. The fight for justice had begun, and it would define the next chapters of my life, shaping not only my career but the very essence of who I am.

Chapter 2:

Building the Movement

The embers of activism, ignited by the fight against the warehouse and fueled by the shared struggles of the Inland Empire community, led to a pivotal next step: the founding of LULAC de Ontario. Our initial meetings were held in borrowed spaces—churches, private homes, and Amy's Farm—reflecting the humble beginnings of an organization born out of necessity. These early gatherings brought together individuals from diverse backgrounds, united by a shared commitment to environmental justice. The discussions were animated, sometimes heated, as we grappled with the complexities of the issues at hand. There was a palpable sense of urgency, a collective understanding that swift and decisive action was needed to address the escalating environmental threats to our community.

One of our earliest challenges was navigating the complex and often hostile political landscape. Local officials, beholden to powerful developers and industrial interests, were unresponsive—sometimes outright dismissive—of our concerns. Meetings were scheduled at inconvenient times, agendas were manipulated, and our voices were routinely ignored. This experience underscored the importance of grassroots mobilization and the need to build a movement capable of exerting real political pressure.

Building consensus within LULAC de Ontario was equally challenging. Our founding members represented a wide spectrum of experiences, perspectives, and priorities. Balancing the needs of different neighborhoods, levels of education, and political experience required careful negotiation and compromise. Passionate debates about strategy, tactics, and long-term goals were common. While these discussions were sometimes fraught with tension, they ultimately strengthened our organization, fostering internal cohesion and broadening our perspective. We learned that diversity, while challenging, was a source of innovation and resilience.

Our early campaigns focused on raising awareness about the environmental hazards impacting our community. We organized educational workshops, distributed flyers detailing the health risks of air and water pollution, and hosted forums where experts shared scientific evidence linking environmental degradation to health problems. We also held community food and toy drives, civic engagement fairs, and voter registration events. These activities not only addressed immediate concerns but also fostered a sense of collective responsibility and ownership.

Working side by side to care for our shared environment strengthened community bonds and created a shared sense of purpose.

One of our most impactful early campaigns centered on preserving agricultural land protected under California's Proposition 70. The South Ontario Logistics Center, a proposed mega-warehouse development, threatened to consume 70 acres of this land and close Amy's Farm, a beloved educational center that taught families about regenerative farming and sustainability. Recognizing the urgency, we mobilized our community, leveraging social media to spread awareness and rally support.

The response was overwhelming—1,100 public comment letters poured in, each a testament to the strength of our collective voice.

This campaign became a turning point for LULAC de Ontario. It demonstrated the power of grassroots organizing and the impact we could achieve when united. It showcased the diverse strengths of our members as we navigated political complexities and stood firm against powerful developers. Through this experience, we refined our strategies, strengthened our unity, and proved that a dedicated group of individuals could make a meaningful difference.

Buoyed by this success, we continued our work with renewed vigor. Each victory, no matter how modest, fueled our resolve and expanded our reach. The campaign to save Amy's Farm became a testament to the power of community and the unwavering spirit of activism that burned brightly within us.

Another critical aspect of our early work was building alliances with other community organizations. We understood that environmental justice was deeply interconnected with other social justice issues, including poverty, inequality, and a lack of access to healthcare. By forging partnerships with groups working on housing, education, and healthcare, we broadened our reach and amplified our collective impact. These coalitions allowed us to leverage the expertise and resources of other organizations, diversifying our approach and strengthening our efforts.

The early years of LULAC de Ontario were marked by a constant tension between maintaining momentum and overcoming internal and external challenges. Funding was perpetually tight, relying heavily on volunteer contributions and small grants. We often operated on a shoestring budget, and the long hours took a toll, leading to burnout and the need for a more sustainable structure. Pushback from powerful interests and bureaucratic obstacles were constant, but these challenges only reinforced the importance of community support and resilience.

Despite the difficulties, we celebrated significant triumphs. Our campaigns raised public awareness, pressured decision-makers, and resulted in tangible improvements in our community's environmental conditions. These victories, though hard-won, proved that grassroots activism could effect meaningful change.

Each success, no matter how small, was celebrated collectively, serving as a beacon of hope and reaffirming our belief in the power of collective action. We learned to value incremental progress, recognizing that large-scale change often requires a series of carefully planned and executed steps.

We also discovered the transformative power of storytelling. Translating complex scientific data into compelling narratives allowed us to engage the public on a deeper level. By sharing personal stories that connected environmental issues to people's daily lives, we transcended political rhetoric and reached audiences emotionally. These authentic accounts highlighted the human cost of environmental degradation, creating a more persuasive and relatable message. We found that people were far more moved by stories of struggle and perseverance than by statistics alone.

As LULAC de Ontario matured, we developed more sophisticated strategies for community engagement. We experimented with different outreach methods, tailoring our messaging to resonate with diverse cultural and linguistic groups. Strengthening ties with local media became a priority, enabling us to amplify our voice and gain broader support for our campaigns. Mastering the art of concise, impactful storytelling has become an integral part of our strategy, enabling us to navigate the media landscape and reach a wider audience.

The founding of LULAC de Ontario was more than the creation of an organization—it was the birth of a movement. It was a testament to the power of community mobilization, the resilience of the human spirit, and the transformative potential of collective action. The journey was arduous, often fraught with challenges and setbacks, but the shared struggles and victories forged an unbreakable bond among our members and with the community. It was a pivotal moment, igniting a movement rooted in integrity and fueled by passion.

We navigated complex political landscapes, stood firm against powerful interests, and built trusted alliances with organizations like EarthJustice, civil rights law firms, the California Attorney General's office, and the Department of Justice. Together, we fought for community rights, amplifying our voices through shared dedication to truth and transparency.

This movement, born from the shared struggles of the Inland Empire, became an unstoppable force. Our early successes, though hard-fought, strengthened our resolve and laid the foundation for a powerful organization. The seeds of change, planted in the fertile ground of the Inland Empire, began to blossom, transforming the landscape and empowering the community to fight for its right to a healthy and sustainable future. The work was far from over, but the foundation had been laid for a movement that would continue to inspire and effect positive change for generations to come.

The momentum generated by LULAC de Ontario's early successes laid the groundwork for broader collaboration. It became increasingly clear that addressing the complex environmental and social justice issues facing the Inland Empire required a unified and strategic approach. This realization led to the formation of the Ontario Future Alliance (OFA), a coalition of diverse organizations and community groups—including NAACP, LULAC, Inland Empire Advocates for the Environment, Princeton Freewill Baptist Church, the Art and Science Cultural Center, Pitzer College Community Engagement Center, University of California Riverside, and M.A.L.O. (Meaning Thank You in Tongan). Together, these groups are committed to building a more sustainable and equitable future for Ontario.

The OFA was designed not as a hierarchical organization but as a collaborative network—a platform where groups could pool resources, share expertise, and amplify their collective voice. The founding members understood the power of synergy, recognizing that by working together, they could achieve far more than they could individually. This collaborative spirit was essential, given the wide range of interconnected issues the alliance sought to address, including environmental protection, affordable housing, access to quality education, and economic development.

Building the OFA was a complex and deliberate process. The initial meetings were vibrant and dynamic, often marked by passionate debates about priorities and strategies.

Consensus-building required patience, compromise, and a commitment to inclusivity, ensuring that all member organizations had a voice in shaping the alliance's direction. Balancing the diverse needs and interests of the groups—each with its own agenda and priorities—demanded skillful mediation and a shared commitment to collaborative problem-solving.

One of the alliance's early challenges was developing a shared vision and strategic plan. Each member organization brought unique expertise and priorities to the table—some focused on environmental protection, others on economic development or social justice. The task was to identify a unifying thread that connected these diverse interests and craft a strategic plan that reflected the broad spectrum of community needs. This required extensive dialogue, negotiation, and compromise, but the result was a comprehensive plan that addressed the interconnected challenges facing the community.

The OFA adopted a multi-pronged approach to tackle these challenges. Its strategic plan outlined key objectives, including improving air and water quality, promoting sustainable development, expanding access to affordable housing and quality education, and creating economic opportunities for residents. Each objective was supported by tailored strategies and action plans, leveraging the unique strengths of the alliance's member organizations.

For example, to address air quality, the OFA collaborated with environmental scientists from local universities to conduct air quality monitoring and analysis. This data informed advocacy efforts, including lobbying for stricter emission standards and promoting cleaner energy technologies. Simultaneously, the alliance worked with community groups to implement educational programs and outreach initiatives, raising public awareness about the health impacts of air pollution. This holistic approach combined scientific research, policy advocacy, and community engagement to drive meaningful change.

Similarly, the alliance tackled affordable housing through a multifaceted strategy. It advocated for increased government funding, partnered with developers to promote affordable housing projects, and organized residents to advocate for their own housing needs. Legal organizations provided assistance to tenants facing eviction, while non-profits offered housing counseling and financial literacy programs. This comprehensive approach addressed housing insecurity from multiple angles, empowering residents and fostering long-term solutions.

Education was another cornerstone of the OFA's work. The alliance partnered with local schools to provide tutoring and mentoring services, improving educational outcomes for disadvantaged students. Workforce development programs were created in collaboration with educational institutions, connecting residents to training opportunities and jobs in emerging green technologies. These efforts went beyond academic support, equipping individuals with the skills and knowledge needed to build brighter futures.

Economic development was also a key priority. The OFA supported local businesses, particularly those with sustainable practices, to create jobs and stimulate economic growth. It facilitated access to capital for small businesses, providing the financial resources needed for expansion. This strategy not only bolstered the local economy but also promoted environmentally responsible business practices.

One of the OFA's most significant achievements was its ability to secure funding for large-scale projects. By pooling resources and presenting a unified front, the alliance significantly increased its chances of obtaining grants and other funding opportunities.

This collective approach enabled the implementation of ambitious projects that would have been unattainable for any single organization.

Despite its successes, the OFA faced considerable challenges. Coordinating a diverse range of groups with differing priorities and organizational cultures required constant negotiation and compromise. Internal disagreements were inevitable, but the alliance's commitment to open communication, regular meetings, and consensus-building helped maintain cohesion. Effective communication was another hurdle. The OFA needed to tailor its messaging to resonate with diverse audiences, including government officials, community residents, businesses, and the media. Utilizing a variety of platforms—social media, local newspapers, community events, and public forums—ensured that its message reached a broad audience.

Sustaining the alliance over the long term required addressing member burnout and fostering a strong organizational culture. The OFA prioritized professional development, skill-building, and creating a sense of community among its members. This mutual support system was essential for maintaining momentum and ensuring the alliance's longevity.

The Ontario Future Alliance demonstrated the transformative potential of collaborative action. Its success lay not only in securing funding and implementing impactful projects but also in building consensus, creating a shared vision, and empowering the community to advocate for its own interests. The OFA became a model for how diverse groups could work together to address complex challenges, fostering a sense of collective responsibility and shared ownership in shaping Ontario's future.

The seeds of change, planted in the rich soil of collaborative activism, began to blossom, transforming Ontario's social and environmental landscape. The alliance's work created a more sustainable and equitable future for its residents, proving that unity and collaboration could overcome even the most daunting challenges. While the journey was far from over, the foundation for lasting change had been firmly established, inspiring hope and determination for the road ahead.

The Ontario Future Alliance (OFA) quickly recognized that its collaborative approach needed to extend beyond physical meetings and traditional outreach methods. The digital revolution, with its ability to facilitate rapid communication and widespread dissemination of information, offered an unprecedented opportunity to amplify their message and engage a broader audience. Leveraging digital media became a cornerstone of the OFA's strategy, transforming their capacity to mobilize support, build consensus, and drive meaningful change.

Initially, the OFA's digital presence was modest. A simple website served as a central hub, providing information about the alliance, its mission, and its activities. Email lists kept members informed about events and developments. However, as the alliance's work expanded, so did its reliance on digital tools. Social media platforms like Facebook, Twitter, and Instagram opened new avenues for communication and engagement, allowing the OFA to bypass traditional media gatekeepers and connect directly with community members.

These platforms enabled the alliance to share updates, mobilize supporters, and foster a sense of community among its diverse membership.

The OFA's strategic use of social media followed a multi-pronged approach. First, they used these platforms to share information about their activities, highlight successes, and disseminate news stories. This steady stream of content kept supporters informed and engaged, ensuring the alliance's message remained visible. They also amplified the voices of community members by featuring personal stories and testimonials, demonstrating the real-world impact of their work. This personalized approach resonated emotionally with audiences, fostering trust and deeper engagement.

Second, social media became a powerful tool for mobilizing support for campaigns and initiatives. The OFA used these platforms to promote events, encourage participation in advocacy efforts, and solicit feedback from the community. Online polls and surveys helped gauge public opinion on key issues, allowing the alliance to adapt its strategies accordingly. For example, during a campaign for stricter environmental regulations, the OFA created a hashtag that quickly went viral, attracting national media attention and generating significant public pressure on local politicians.

Third, digital platforms fostered a sense of community and shared purpose among the OFA's diverse membership. Online forums and discussion groups provided spaces for members to connect, share ideas, and collaborate on projects. These virtual spaces allowed for flexible communication, enabling members to participate at their convenience—an essential feature for busy volunteers who couldn't always attend in-person meetings. This approach strengthened bonds within the alliance and enhanced collaboration across geographically dispersed members.

However, transitioning to a more digitally focused strategy presented unique challenges. Maintaining a consistent online presence requires dedicated resources and expertise, including staff or volunteers to manage social media accounts, create content, and respond to comments and inquiries. The OFA had to navigate the complexities of online communication, including managing negative feedback and addressing criticism professionally. Recognizing the need for a robust digital strategy, the alliance invested in training to equip members with the necessary skills and established clear guidelines to ensure all online interactions reflected their values of inclusivity and respect.

Another challenge was ensuring their digital outreach reached a diverse and representative audience. The OFA understood that not everyone had equal access to the internet or the same level of digital literacy. To address this, they adopted a multi-channel approach, combining online efforts with traditional outreach methods such as in-person events, local newspapers, and radio broadcasts. They also translated online content into multiple languages to ensure accessibility for all community members.

The OFA prioritized accuracy and credibility in their online communication. In an era of misinformation, building trust with their audience was paramount. They implemented fact-checking processes, cited reliable sources, and provided accurate contact information to maintain transparency. This commitment to responsible communication helped establish the OFA as a trustworthy and reliable voice in the community.

Adapting to the ever-evolving digital landscape was another ongoing challenge. Social media algorithms, user preferences, and technological advancements necessitated the OFA to continually refine its strategies. They actively monitored online conversations, analyzed engagement metrics, and adjusted their content to align with audience interests and preferences. This adaptability ensured their digital efforts remained effective and impactful.

Beyond information dissemination and campaign promotion, digital media played a pivotal role in building relationships with key stakeholders. The OFA's strong online presence showcased their credibility, expertise, and commitment, attracting the attention of policymakers, business leaders, and other influential individuals who supported their initiatives. Digital tools also enhanced collaboration among the alliance's member organizations, providing efficient ways to share documents, discuss strategies, and track project progress. This streamlined communication improved coordination and synergy across the diverse coalition.

The OFA's experience demonstrated the transformative power of digital media in building and sustaining a successful social movement. By strategically leveraging these tools, they expanded their reach, amplified their message, and engaged a broader audience. However, their journey also highlighted the importance of careful planning, effective resource allocation, and a commitment to the ethical and responsible use of digital platforms. Their approach offers valuable lessons for other activist groups seeking to harness the power of digital media to achieve their goals.

The OFA's success lay in its ability to combine online and offline strategies, ensuring inclusivity while building trust and credibility. Their use of digital tools not only connected and organized people across geographical boundaries but also transformed their ability to mobilize and drive significant social and environmental change. The alliance's story stands as a testament to the power of collaborative action, enhanced and amplified through digital innovation, in forging lasting change within a community. Their example serves as a compelling case study of how modern activism can thrive in the digital age, inspiring others to harness technology in the fight for justice and equity.

My approach to community engagement for environmental justice initiatives was multifaceted, rooted in the understanding that effective outreach goes beyond simply sharing information. It was about building relationships, fostering trust, and empowering individuals to actively participate in the movement. This required a nuanced understanding of the community's demographics, cultural dynamics, and existing social networks.

A key starting point was identifying influential community leaders—not necessarily those in formal positions, but individuals with significant social capital who could mobilize others.

Building rapport with these trusted leaders was essential, as they served as bridges to wider segments of the population. I engaged in regular dialogue with them, seeking their input on campaign strategies, addressing their concerns, and building consensus around shared goals.

This collaborative approach ensured that initiatives aligned with the community's values and priorities, avoiding the pitfalls of imposing externally driven agendas.

Beyond engaging leaders, grassroots outreach was a cornerstone of our strategy. We organized community events such as workshops, town hall meetings, and educational forums. These gatherings served multiple purposes: they provided platforms to share information about environmental issues, highlighted the local impact, and showcased successful case studies from other regions. Just as importantly, they fostered a sense of shared identity and collective action. Participants were encouraged to voice their concerns, share their experiences, and contribute ideas, creating a sense of empowerment and ownership over the movement.

Inclusivity and accessibility were central to enhancing participation. Events were held in easily accessible locations, ensuring they were open to all community members regardless of physical ability or socioeconomic status. Materials were translated into multiple languages to reflect the community's linguistic diversity.

We also employed a variety of communication formats—presentations, interactive workshops, and informal discussions—

to cater to different learning styles and preferences. Recognizing that not everyone felt comfortable in large group settings, we facilitated smaller, more intimate gatherings, creating safe spaces for individuals to share their perspectives without feeling overwhelmed.

Our strategy extended beyond in-person engagement to leverage the power of digital media. A dedicated website served as a central hub for up-to-date information on campaigns, resources, and opportunities for involvement. Social media platforms like Facebook, Twitter, and Instagram allowed us to share updates, inspiring stories, and calls to action, reaching a broader audience and overcoming geographical barriers.

My team managed these platforms diligently, responding promptly to comments and inquiries to foster a sense of responsiveness and engagement. Compelling visuals, short videos, and digestible content ensured our message resonated with diverse demographics while avoiding information overload. The online presence also showcased the movement's successes, inspiring others to join the cause.

However, community engagement was not without its challenges. One significant hurdle was overcoming skepticism and distrust, particularly toward government-led initiatives or externally funded campaigns. To address this, we emphasized transparency and accountability. Financial reports were made publicly available, and regular updates on campaign progress were shared.

We prioritized collaboration with existing community organizations, demonstrating a commitment to working alongside, rather than for, the community. This partnership-based approach fostered trust and a sense of shared ownership, mitigating concerns about outside influences. Building these relationships required consistent effort, active listening, and a genuine commitment to addressing community concerns.

Another challenge was navigating the diversity of opinions within the community. Not everyone shared the same level of concern about environmental issues, and some held conflicting views on the best course of action. We addressed these differences through open dialogue and respectful communication, focusing on finding common ground rather than engaging in confrontation.

We actively sought out dissenting voices, acknowledging their perspectives and exploring ways to incorporate their concerns into our strategies. This inclusive approach ensured the movement felt representative of the entire community, strengthening its legitimacy and appeal. It wasn't about appeasing dissent but about understanding its roots and fostering constructive engagement.

Ensuring equitable access to information and resources was another significant challenge. To address this, we collaborated with local libraries and community centers to provide access to computers and internet services for those lacking digital connectivity. We organized workshops to improve digital literacy, empowering individuals to engage more fully with online resources and platforms. Additionally, we employed diverse outreach methods—printed materials, radio announcements, and community events—to ensure information reached people through their preferred channels, regardless of technological access.

Celebrating successes was a vital component of sustaining momentum. Acknowledging community contributions, highlighting achievements, and sharing inspiring stories of progress reinforced the collective sense of purpose. Celebrations, whether large public events or smaller community gatherings, boosted morale and demonstrated the tangible impact of collective action. These milestones served as evidence of progress, fostering a sense of efficacy and encouraging continued engagement.

Our experience demonstrated that successful community engagement for environmental justice requires a long-term commitment to building trust, fostering dialogue, and empowering individuals. It is not a quick fix but a continuous process of relationship-building, adaptation, and responsive communication. Inclusivity, accessibility, and transparency were critical to creating a movement that was both effective and sustainable.

The success of our initiatives underscored the importance of understanding community dynamics and investing in genuine engagement. The enduring impact of our work lies not only in the environmental achievements but also in the empowerment and sustained participation of the community itself. By fostering trust, inclusivity, and shared ownership, we created a foundation for lasting change—one that continues to inspire and drive progress toward environmental justice.

The path to environmental justice, even with a carefully crafted strategy, was far from smooth. Resistance—both overt and subtle—emerged from various quarters. One significant hurdle was the entrenched skepticism among some community members toward external initiatives, particularly those perceived as government-driven or corporate-funded.

Despite our emphasis on transparency and collaboration with local organizations, suspicions lingered. Some viewed the environmental justice movement as an imposition, disconnected from the immediate concerns of poverty, unemployment, and access to basic services. Overcoming this skepticism required consistent and patient dialogue, along with a demonstrable commitment to addressing the community's broader needs.

This realization prompted a shift in strategy. We moved beyond advocating solely for environmental protection to integrating environmental concerns into the community's existing struggles.

By connecting environmental issues to economic development, public health, and social justice, we demonstrated tangible benefits that extended beyond the abstract notion of a cleaner environment.

For instance, campaigns to remediate contaminated land were tied to job creation in sustainable industries, showcasing the economic empowerment potential of environmental restoration. Similarly, efforts to improve air quality were linked to public health initiatives, emphasizing the direct connection between pollution and respiratory illnesses. This strategic integration helped build a broader coalition of support, uniting diverse community interests around shared goals.

Another major obstacle was the active opposition from vested interests. Industrial polluters, reluctant to adopt stricter environmental regulations, worked to undermine the movement through lobbying, misinformation campaigns, and attempts to discredit its leaders. In response, we meticulously documented environmental violations, pursued legal action to hold polluters accountable, and leveraged media exposure to highlight their harmful practices. This required significant investments in legal expertise and media relations, further stretching our already limited resources.

Financial constraints presented a persistent challenge. Securing sustainable funding was an ongoing struggle, with grants often falling short of the movement's needs. The constant search for new funding sources diverted time and energy from core community engagement efforts, creating a delicate balancing act between fundraising and on-the-ground activism. This financial precariousness left the movement vulnerable to setbacks and underscored the urgency of securing stable resources.

Even within the movement's supportive core, internal disagreements occasionally surfaced. The diversity of views and interests within the community sometimes led to conflicts over campaign strategies and the allocation of resources. Navigating these tensions required careful mediation, compromise, and a commitment to inclusive decision-making. We fostered a culture of open communication, ensuring all voices were heard and respected, even when disagreements arose. This process demanded active listening, empathy, and a willingness to adjust strategies based on community input.

In the face of these challenges, the resilience of both the coalition and the community proved essential. Our unwavering commitment, coupled with the ability to adapt strategies and build alliances, became the foundation of the movement's success. We learned to leverage small victories—such as the cleanup of a polluted site, the passage of a local ordinance, or increased participation in a community event—to build momentum and inspire further engagement. Celebrating these achievements, no matter how modest, served as vital morale boosters, demonstrating the tangible impact of collective action.

The community's resilience was equally remarkable. Despite facing environmental injustices, financial hardships, and internal conflicts, they persevered with an unwavering commitment to the cause. The sense of shared identity and collective purpose fostered through years of engagement strategies proved invaluable in sustaining the movement during difficult times. The relationships built through collaboration provided a vital support system, enabling the community to weather setbacks and continue their fight for environmental justice.

A critical element in overcoming these hurdles was a commitment to continuous learning and adaptation. We regularly evaluated our strategies, sought feedback from community members, and adjusted our approach as needed. Recognizing that the dynamics of the movement were constantly evolving, we embraced flexibility and a willingness to learn from both successes and failures. This iterative approach involved analyzing engagement metrics, conducting feedback sessions with community leaders, and reviewing campaign strategies after events. These evaluations allowed us to identify areas for improvement and make informed decisions about future actions.

Another key to building resilience was cultivating strong leadership within the community. We invested heavily in empowering community members to take on leadership roles, offering training and mentorship opportunities to build their capacity for advocacy and organizing. This distributed leadership model ensured the movement wasn't dependent on a single individual, enhancing its sustainability. Training programs included workshops on community organizing, communication skills, public speaking, and media engagement.

Mentorship programs paired experienced activists with newer members, fostering knowledge transfer and organically developing leadership skills.

Storytelling emerged as a powerful tool in sustaining the movement's resilience. Sharing personal stories of environmental injustice, highlighting the impact on individuals and families, and celebrating stories of perseverance helped maintain community engagement and inspire action. These narratives created a collective sense of identity and purpose, fueling the movement's momentum. Storytelling wasn't limited to formal presentations; it also occurred in informal settings—such as community gatherings, online forums, and personal conversations—creating a pervasive sense of shared experience and solidarity.

Ultimately, overcoming these obstacles and building resilience hinged on establishing deep trust and mutual respect between the coalition and the community. Years of sustained engagement, transparent communication, and collaborative decision-making created a strong foundation for the movement to withstand challenges. This trust wasn't transactional; it was a genuine partnership built on shared values and a commitment to achieving common goals. The strength of this partnership proved to be the most significant factor in overcoming adversity and building a sustainable movement for environmental justice.

The ongoing success of the movement stands as a testament to the power of collective action, resilience, and a steadfast commitment to environmental and social justice. It demonstrated that genuine community engagement—rooted in respect, inclusivity, and mutual understanding—is not just a strategy but the foundation upon which lasting change is built.

Chapter 3:

Addressing Key Issues

The Inland Empire, a sprawling region encompassing parts of Riverside and San Bernardino counties in Southern California, has long grappled with significant air and water pollution challenges. Decades of industrial activity, coupled with rapid population growth and sprawling urbanization, have contributed to a complex environmental crisis demanding multifaceted solutions. Addressing this pollution required a robust scientific foundation, meticulously documenting the extent of the problem and establishing a clear causal link between specific pollutants and their adverse effects on public health and the environment.

This involved leveraging existing air quality monitoring data from the South Coast Air Quality Management District (SCAQMD), a regional agency responsible for regulating air pollution in Southern California, and gathering and analyzing data from CalEnviroScreen. Data analysis revealed alarmingly high levels of particulate matter (PM2.5 and PM10), ozone, and various toxic air contaminants, significantly exceeding acceptable thresholds established by the Environmental Protection Agency (EPA) and California Air Resources Board (CARB). These pollutants, often originating from industrial sources, vehicle emissions, and agricultural practices, were directly linked to increased rates of respiratory illnesses, cardiovascular diseases, and other health problems within the Inland Empire's communities. Studies conducted by local universities and public health agencies corroborated this data, reinforcing the urgency of intervention.

Beyond air quality, water pollution posed another severe threat. Runoff from agricultural fields, industrial discharge, and inadequate wastewater treatment infrastructure contaminated local waterways, impacting both human health and the delicate ecosystem. Testing revealed high levels of nitrates, pesticides, and other harmful substances in rivers, streams, and groundwater supplies, posing a risk to drinking water quality and aquatic life. This scientific evidence, meticulously compiled and presented, provided the compelling case for action.

The strategy to tackle pollution in the Inland Empire encompassed a multi-pronged approach, involving legal action, collaborative partnerships, and community-based initiatives. Legal battles became a crucial component, targeting major polluters who consistently violated environmental regulations. Lawsuits filed against industrial facilities responsible for significant air and water pollution leveraged the scientific evidence compiled, demanding stricter compliance with existing laws and seeking remediation of past environmental damage. These legal actions, while resource-intensive, proved essential in holding polluters accountable and pushing for meaningful changes. The success of these lawsuits became a landmark achievement, paving the way for subsequent legal challenges against other polluting industries within the region. Further, these cases set a legal precedent that served as a deterrent against future environmental violations.

Simultaneously, fostering collaborations with government agencies became paramount. This involved working closely with the SCAQMD, CARB, and other relevant agencies to implement stricter emission standards, enhance monitoring efforts, and develop comprehensive pollution control strategies. Collaboration with the California Department of Water Resources (DWR) focused on improving water infrastructure, reducing agricultural runoff, and enhancing wastewater treatment capabilities. These partnerships, built on trust and shared goals, proved vital in securing additional resources, technical expertise, and regulatory support to tackle the region's environmental challenges. The collaborative efforts transcended purely bureaucratic engagement; they also involved joint public awareness campaigns, aimed at informing the public about the sources of pollution and the potential risks to public health.

Community-based initiatives formed the third crucial pillar of the pollution reduction strategy. Recognizing the importance of community engagement and local participation, a substantial effort was made to empower local residents and build their capacity to participate in environmental protection. This involved establishing environmental education programs in local schools, conducting community workshops, and organizing citizen science projects. These programs encouraged community members to monitor air and water quality in their neighborhoods actively, collecting data and reporting environmental violations. This participatory approach fostered a sense of ownership and responsibility, empowering residents to become active participants in environmental protection efforts. The data collected by community members was incorporated into the larger scientific data set, providing valuable local context and enhancing the overall accuracy of the pollution assessment.

Further, community-led initiatives focused on developing sustainable practices within the region. These included promoting the use of public transportation, encouraging the adoption of cleaner vehicle technologies, and supporting local businesses committed to sustainable practices. Community gardens were established, fostering a connection between local residents and sustainable food production, thereby reducing reliance on industrial agriculture and its associated environmental impacts. These gardens also served as educational hubs, promoting environmental awareness and providing opportunities for community members to engage in hands-on environmental stewardship. The involvement of community organizations, local leaders, and faith-based groups fostered a collective commitment to creating a healthier and more sustainable environment, demonstrating that environmental justice was intricately intertwined with economic opportunity and community empowerment.

The impact of these multi-faceted strategies was demonstrable. Over time, air and water quality gradually improved. Levels of PM2.5 and other harmful pollutants decreased, leading to improvements in public health indicators. Respiratory illnesses and other health problems linked to air pollution showed a decline, although the improvement remained uneven across different socioeconomic groups within the Inland Empire. Similarly, water quality improved in many areas, with reductions in nitrates and other contaminants. While challenges remain, the success in reducing pollution underscores the transformative potential of a comprehensive strategy that blends scientific rigor, legal action, collaborative partnerships, and community engagement. The positive changes achieved stand as a testament to the efficacy of sustained commitment and demonstrate the long-term benefits of collaborative environmental stewardship. This success story showcases a model that can be replicated in other regions struggling with similar environmental issues, highlighting the importance of sustained investment in environmental protection and community empowerment.

However, the journey was not without its obstacles. Funding limitations persistently hampered the implementation of certain initiatives. Securing sufficient funding for environmental remediation, legal battles, and community education programs often proved challenging. The need for continued advocacy and securing grants from both public and private sources became a continuous effort. The need to navigate complex regulatory processes and bureaucratic hurdles also added further layers of complexity. Despite these challenges, the commitment to protecting the environment persisted. The resilience of the community, fueled by their direct experience of environmental injustice, proved invaluable in overcoming these hurdles.

Looking ahead, sustained vigilance remains crucial. Environmental monitoring and enforcement efforts must be intensified to ensure that improvements are maintained. Further, new challenges, such as climate change and its impact on air and water quality, demand proactive adaptation. The success achieved demonstrates that the fight for environmental justice requires sustained commitment, continuous adaptation, funding, and the unwavering belief in collective action. The lessons learned in the Inland Empire provide a valuable blueprint for other regions grappling with similar environmental issues, reminding us that a healthy environment is not merely an environmental concern but a fundamental prerequisite for public health, social equity, and economic prosperity.

Amy felt a chill despite the summer heat, a premonition clinging to her like the humid air. The tomatoes, usually a source of joy, felt heavy with unspoken sorrow.

A distant tractor rumbled, a mournful sound that mirrored the anxiety in her heart. This year's harvest felt different, threatened by something unseen.

The weight of responsibility pressed down; the farm, her family's legacy, seemed fragile. Could she save it, or was this the end? A heavy sorrow hung in the air, a shared lament from the 1,100 of us who had passionately dedicated ourselves to preserving this final remnant of Ontario's agrarian heritage. At the Ontario City Council meeting, our unified presence—a powerful demonstration of support for Amy and her father's business—was a testament to our fervent efforts to assist Amy in her fight to retain her farm.

"This isn't just about a farm, folks," I said, addressing the crowd gathered outside City Hall that chilly March evening. My voice, usually steady, trembled slightly. "It's about our children, our history, our future." The biting wind whipped around us, mirroring the anxieties in our hearts. We fought for more than just acres; we fought for community.

Amy's legacy, and the future of similar farms, hung precariously in the balance. Our collective voice demanded preservation. This struggle represented a larger battle against encroaching urbanization, a fight for the soul of our town. The council's decision loomed large.

During this fight, the developers heard about the coalition of resistance I had formed, and got on a flight the next day. The developers had contacted LULAC and arranged a meeting with me at a local hotel located near the Ontario airport. The air in the hotel room crackled with the stench of desperation and stale coffee. Their offer – a crisp, cold $200,000 – felt like a slap in the face. These developers, slick and oily, thought they could buy my silence, buy the silence of my community. They thought they could buy me. Their words slithered across the table, each syllable a venomous insect. "Shut up," they hissed, the implication dripping with contempt. "Walk away." My response was a single word, a granite wall against their tide of corruption: "No." The taste of defiance was sharp, metallic on my tongue. I felt the weight of 1,100 voices – my community – pressing down on me, a silent army demanding justice. The developer's relentless calls to the LULAC Directors, their attempts to circumvent me, felt like a physical assault. Each ring, a viper striking at the heart of our organization. As President and Founder of LULAC de Ontario, I slammed the phone down on each attempt, the sound echoing the unwavering resolve in my soul. No negotiation. No compromise. They didn't understand. They couldn't grasp the burning injustice of it all – their greed pitted against the sacred ground of Amy, her father, and our community's beloved farm and cultural center. The developers wanted to bulldoze our history, erase our heritage. But they underestimated the fierce loyalty that binds us. The land, scarred but resilient, was our lifeblood. If anyone was to receive compensation, it would be those who deserved it – Amy, her father, and the community. We would rebuild, protect, and reclaim what was ours, and their blood money would remain untouched, a monument to their failed attempt to buy my soul. For me, it wasn't about the money, it was about principle.

Standing true to my core values and beliefs in order to be the light upon the hill, to lead by example. To be the beacon of hope that would never betray my community, the land, my home.

During the developer's attempts to silence me, we, the newly formed LULAC de Ontario Council, had tirelessly fought to save the last place for parents and teachers to create memories with their children. We'd organized, strategized, and spent weeks collecting signatures. Each email echoed the desperate plea: Don't let them pave paradise and put up a parking lot - a massive warehouse, to be precise - over 200 acres of protected agricultural land. Amy's Farm was our heart, like a precious seed that we nurtured to teach children about regenerative farming and ecosystems.

"My son learned to respect the land at Amy's," Mrs. Rodriguez, a woman with eyes that held the weight of generations, whispered to me. "He learned about life, about responsibility, about where his food comes from. They can't just take that away from us."

Her words mirrored sentiments echoed in hundreds of letters we'd submitted. One, from a school teacher, described how Amy's Farm was the only place her students could experience the life cycle of plants and animals, firsthand. Another spoke of family traditions, of generations who had connected with the land on those very fields. Each comment painted a vivid picture of a community deeply rooted in its agricultural heritage, a heritage now under threat.

The meeting itself was a chilling display of powerlessness. The council members, seated on their elevated dais, seemed to regard our pleas with detached formality. One even joked about the "traffic congestion" Amy's Farm might cause. The final vote? 5-0 in favor of the warehouse project.

"They ignored us," Farmer Randy, owner and operator of Amy's Farm, an older, gentleman dressed in cowboy gear, spat out after the meeting. His face was contorted with a mixture of anger and despair. "1,100 comments! And they didn't even flinch." Amy stood still as she looked over at her father, Farmer Randy, the weight of defeat settling over them. The vibrant community that had rallied behind her now felt like a distant dream. The council's decision echoed in her and her father's minds, a stark reminder of the fragile nature of their existence. As darkness fell, a somber appreciation dinner concluded, yet a palpable sense of dread clung to Amy as she left the celebratory table. The moon, a spectral orb, cast an unsettling glow upon the fields, lands her family had cultivated for countless years, now tinged with the bitter taste of farewell. The air was thick with the buzz of insects, a familiar comfort in an uncertain time. As she passed the old oak tree, a figure emerged from the shadows. It was Mrs. Rodriguez, her eyes shining with a mixture of determination and sorrow. "We may have lost this battle, Amy, but the war isn't over yet. We won't let their warehouses steal the heart of our community." Her words, spoken with conviction, kindled a spark of hope in Amy's heart. Together, they stood, refusing to let the darkness consume them, knowing that their fight for the land and their legacy would continue.

The lawsuit that followed was a brutal, grinding fight. I fought hard, rallying the community, leveraging every legal recourse available to make one last attempt at helping Farmer Randy and his daughter, Amy save the farm. But the developers held significant sway. In the end, a partial victory – a Pyrrhic one, really – was all we could claim. Seventy acres were preserved, enough to relocate Amy's Farm, albeit on a drastically reduced scale that caused the cultural center to close down.

Amy, her face etched with exhaustion but her spirit unbroken, told me, "It's not what it was, but it's something. We can still grow food, keep the family legacy alive, but for what?

Everything we worked hard to build over the last 30 years gone overnight." The community rallied, donating time and resources to help rebuild, a testament to Amy's dedication. Yet, the shadow of loss hung heavy. The smaller farm meant fewer jobs, impacting the local economy. Amy's legacy continues, but at a devastating cost. The fight for the remaining land continues; the developers eye the adjacent properties, threatening further encroachment.

The reduced size means a significant decrease in food production, and no capacity to care for farm animals. The vibrant community hub, the lively space where children learned and families connected, was gone, reduced to nothing. The massive loss hung heavy on my shoulders, the weight of the community's collective grief compounded by the council's blatant disregard for our concerns. Yet, even in the face of this defeat, the resilience of the community, our determination to preserve even a sliver of what we held dear, remains our testament – a small, stubborn blossom pushing through the cracked pavement. The fight for Ontario's agricultural legacy, it seems, continues.

The fight for environmental justice in the Inland Empire extended beyond air and water quality to encompass a critical social determinant of health: housing. The region, experiencing rapid population growth and economic shifts, grappled with a severe housing crisis. "It's a nightmare," Councilwoman Leslie Alvarez stated at a recent city council meeting. "Families are being forced out of their homes, rents are skyrocketing, and we're not building nearly enough affordable units to keep up." The shortage disproportionately affected low-income families, communities of color, and vulnerable populations, exacerbating existing social and economic disparities. The lack of access to safe, stable, and affordable housing contributed significantly to health problems, educational setbacks, and economic instability. Addressing this crisis required a comprehensive strategy.

Our initial efforts focused on documenting the crisis's extent. We collaborated with local housing agencies, conducting detailed surveys and analyzing census data. "The numbers were staggering," reported Jose Ramirez, director of the Inland Empire Housing for Justice

Coalition, at a nonprofit roundtable. "Our surveys showed thousands of families facing eviction, overcrowding, and substandard conditions. I spoke to one mother, a single parent working two jobs, who was facing eviction because her rent had increased by 40%." Local chapters of other housing nonprofits provided invaluable on-the-ground data and insights. "We see the desperation firsthand," shared Anthony Garcia, a housing for Justice Coalition volunteer. "Families are sacrificing food and medicine just to keep a roof over their heads." The data painted a grim picture: the lack of affordable rental units drove up costs, forcing many families to spend a disproportionate share of their income on housing, leaving little for other necessities.

Armed with this data, we began advocating for policy changes. "We had to fight for every inch," recalled Councilman David Lee. "At the city council meetings, we faced resistance from developers who prioritized profit over people. But we had the data, and we had the community on our side." This involved working with elected officials, drafting legislation, and mobilizing community support for policies aimed at increasing the supply of affordable housing, protecting tenants' rights, and preventing displacement. "We pushed for increased funding for affordable housing programs," explained Sarah Chen, a community organizer. "At one state legislative hearing, I testified about a family I knew, forced to live in a motel after losing their home. Their story brought the issue to life for the lawmakers." We advocated for the California Housing Trust Fund and local community development block grants, and pushed for inclusionary zoning policies. This often involved intense lobbying efforts and navigating complex bureaucratic processes. "It wasn't easy," admitted Councilman Lee. "But seeing the impact of our work on families – that's what keeps us going." Public forums were crucial for educating policymakers and the public. "We had to show people that affordable housing isn't just a social issue; it's a public health crisis," stated Dr. Ramirez, a public health official, during a community forum. "The lack of safe and affordable housing has a devastating impact on people's health and well-being."

Beyond advocacy, we prioritized strengthening tenant protections. "At the last city council meeting," Councilwoman Alvarez recounted, "I pushed hard for the stricter rent control measures, and I'm glad to say we finally got them passed. It was a long fight, but hearing directly from tenants facing eviction – one woman told me she was just one missed paycheck away from losing everything – made the struggle worthwhile." We lobbied for expanded eviction protections, and strengthened the enforcement of existing housing codes. "The existing codes were toothless," Maria Sanchez, a community organizer with Tenants United, shared at a recent nonprofit roundtable. "We needed stronger enforcement, and the fines for landlords violating the codes needed to be substantial. Now, there's finally some accountability."

We worked closely with tenant rights organizations, assisting tenants facing eviction or unfair housing practices. "We had a case just last month," John Houston, a paralegal with the Legal Aid Society, explained. "A family was facing wrongful eviction. We used the newly strengthened laws to get them back in their home and ensure the landlord paid penalties." We organized workshops and educational campaigns to empower tenants with the knowledge of their rights and the resources available to them. "The workshops were a game-changer," one participant, a young mother named Aisha, shared in a post-workshop survey. "I learned I had rights I never knew existed. I finally felt empowered to stand up for myself." These initiatives proved vital in mitigating displacement and ensuring that vulnerable families were not further marginalized by housing insecurity.

Recognizing that policy changes alone were insufficient, we also implemented community-based housing initiatives. "The community land trust model is a key part of our long-term strategy," Mayor Thompson stated at a press conference. "It ensures affordability for generations to come." We supported the development of community land trusts, which allow for the permanent affordability of housing units. "The cooperative model allows us to truly put residents in the driver's seat," explained Michael Tupou, a member of the newly formed cooperative housing board. "We're not just tenants, we're owners, responsible for our own community." We facilitated the creation of cooperative housing models, empowering residents to collectively own and manage their housing. These approaches fostered community ownership and control over housing resources, promoting long-term affordability and community stability. We also actively supported the construction of new affordable housing units through collaborations with non-profit developers and the utilization of innovative financing mechanisms, including tax credits and public-private partnerships. "Securing those tax credits was a huge victory," noted Sarah Miller, executive director of Affordable Housing Now. "It wouldn't have happened without the city council's support and the tireless work of our coalition." These initiatives often faced significant challenges. Securing funding for affordable housing projects remained a major hurdle, as competition for limited public funds was intense. "The budget process is brutal," admitted Councilman Alvarez during a budget hearing. "Everyone wants a piece of the pie, and affordable housing often gets squeezed."

We encountered resistance from developers and property owners who prioritized market-rate housing, hindering the expansion of affordable housing options. "Some developers just see dollar signs," commented one resident at a public forum. "They don't care about the community, only profit." Navigating the complex regulatory environment, characterized by lengthy approval processes and stringent building codes, often resulted in protracted delays. "The bureaucratic red tape is insane," one frustrated non-profit developer shared at a roundtable. "It takes years to get a project approved." Furthermore, overcoming NIMBYism (Not In My Backyard) sentiments from some residents resistant to new affordable housing developments posed a significant obstacle. "We had to address the fears and concerns of the community," explained Pastor Johnson, a community leader instrumental in bridging the gap between residents and developers. "We held numerous town halls, showing that this new housing wasn't just good for those in need but beneficial to the whole neighborhood." Addressing these challenges required creative solutions, strategic alliances, and unwavering community engagement.

Despite these challenges, we witnessed tangible progress. We secured significant investments in affordable housing programs, resulting in the construction of hundreds of new affordable housing units across the Inland Empire. Our advocacy efforts led to strengthened tenant protections, preventing many families from facing eviction and homelessness. The community-based housing initiatives fostered a sense of community ownership and empowerment, strengthening social cohesion and fostering resilience. The success of these programs demonstrated that a multi-pronged approach, combining policy reform, community mobilization, and strategic partnerships, was essential to making a meaningful impact on the housing crisis.

However, the housing crisis remains a complex and evolving issue. The ongoing effects of economic inequality, coupled with the increasing cost of living and the ongoing climate crisis, are factors that continue to worsen the situation. The need for affordable housing continues to outpace available resources. The challenge moving forward involves building upon the successes achieved while addressing the new and emergent challenges that continue to arise. Sustained commitment and creative adaptation are crucial to achieving long-term solutions that create equitable access to safe, stable, and affordable housing for all members of the Inland Empire community. The struggle for housing justice, intrinsically linked to environmental justice and social equity, remains a vital component in the broader fight for a more just and sustainable society. The ongoing work of advocacy, community organizing, and policy change remains paramount in advancing the cause of affordable housing and creating communities where all residents can thrive.

The lessons learned from addressing the housing crisis underscore the importance of data-driven decision-making, the power of community organizing, and the need for collaborative partnerships among government agencies, non-profit organizations, and community residents. The fight for adequate housing is an ongoing one, demanding

sustained vigilance, creative solutions, and a deep commitment to social justice. It is a fight that demands the collaborative energy of all stakeholders in the Inland Empire and exemplifies the interconnectedness of environmental, social, and economic justice. The successful strategies implemented in the Inland Empire provide a model that can be replicated and adapted in other communities facing similar challenges, proving that collective action can achieve meaningful and sustainable progress toward creating a more equitable and just society. The struggle for housing justice is far from over, but the gains made provide a foundation for continued progress, demonstrating that even the most deeply entrenched problems can be tackled through strategic planning, collaborative efforts, and a commitment to social justice and environmental sustainability.

The fight for environmental and housing justice in the Inland Empire naturally bled into another crucial battleground: education. "It's all connected," Ada Sanchez, a local School Board President, told me during one of our countless meetings. "Poverty, pollution, and poor schools – they all reinforce each other."

Eileen Martinez, a fellow school board member, nodded in agreement. "I see it firsthand in my own district," she confided, her voice laced with weariness. "Kids coming to school hungry, lacking basic supplies, their parents burdened by unstable housing and low-wage jobs. How can they focus on learning?"

Our initial task was daunting: documenting the sheer scale of the educational disparities. We spent months poring over data – test scores, graduation rates, suspension rates, resource allocation – the numbers painting a stark picture. School Board member, Richard Montanez, shook his head as he reviewed the spreadsheets. "These discrepancies are criminal," he muttered, pointing to a graph illustrating the vast funding gap between affluent and low-income schools.

"It's not just about funding, though," a community organizer, Heather Hernandez, emphasized during a public forum. "It's about the quality of teachers, the resources available, the feeling of safety and belonging within the school walls." Her words resonated with many parents present. One mother, Elena Rodriguez, shared her frustration: "My daughter's school is overcrowded, the classrooms are falling apart, and they barely have any books. How can they expect her to succeed?"

"We need to make sure every child, regardless of their zip code, has access to a quality education," I heard Ada Sanchez declare forcefully at a legislative hearing. "This isn't just a matter of fairness; it's an investment in our future."

The lobbying process was a grueling marathon. We faced resistance from legislators who prioritized other budget items. "Education is important, but we have limited resources," a state senator explained dismissively, a statement that echoed repeatedly through the chambers. But we persevered, building coalitions with teacher unions, community organizations, and even some unlikely allies. Eileen Martinez, ever the strategist, skillfully navigated the political landscape, forging alliances and swaying opinions.

Securing funding was only half the battle. We also had to tackle the issue of school infrastructure. "The schools in these low-income communities are a disgrace," Richard Montanez exclaimed during a site visit to a dilapidated school. "The buildings are crumbling, the technology is outdated, and it's simply not a safe or conducive environment for learning." The community echoed his sentiments. One teacher, Mr. Reeves, shared, "I love my students, but the conditions here are demoralizing. It's nearly impossible to provide quality teaching with crumbling classrooms and lack of basic resources."

The path to educational equity was long and arduous, fraught with political maneuvering and bureaucratic hurdles. Yet, witnessing the collective efforts of school board members, community activists, educators, and parents ignited a shared determination. The fight was far from over, but the seeds of change were sown, a collective yearning for a more just and equitable future resonating through the Inland Empire.

Improving teacher quality was, as we all know, the elephant in the room. "We need to make teaching a more attractive profession," Ms. Rodriguez, a board member, stated forcefully during one particularly heated meeting. I heard her words reverberate through the tense silence, reflecting the frustration shared by many. Mr. Jones, a community member and father of two, nodded grimly. "My daughter's class has had three different teachers this year. It's unacceptable." His voice, raw with exhaustion, spoke volumes.

The teacher shortage, particularly in underserved areas, was a relentless pressure point. "My son's school is overcrowded," another parent, Mrs. Fuamatu, confided in me during a parent-teacher conference. "The teachers are clearly overwhelmed. It's not fair to them, and it's certainly not fair to the children." Her words resonated deeply, echoing the concerns of many parents I interacted with. Even among the board members, there was a palpable tension. "We need to increase salaries," argued Mr. Caballero, another board member, "but where is the money going to come from?" The question hung heavy in the air, a stark reminder of the budget constraints.

We advocated for policies, but their implementation was fraught with challenges. "The bureaucratic red tape is killing us," one exasperated teacher, Ms. Fuamatu, confided. "It takes months just to get approval for new materials." Her frustration highlighted the disconnect between policy and practice. Meanwhile, the board members grappled with the political complexities. "We can't just throw money at the problem," countered Ms.

Rodriguez. "We need sustainable solutions." Her voice, though measured, betrayed her anxieties about long-term funding.

Parental engagement was another key area. "The workshops were incredibly helpful," one parent shared. "I finally understand how the school system works." However, another parent expressed frustration. "It's hard to find time to attend these things, especially if you're working multiple jobs." This feedback illuminated the practical barriers to participation. The board members were keenly aware of this. "We need to make these resources more accessible," Ms. Rodriguez asserted. "Perhaps offer online options or evening sessions." Her suggestion reflected a growing understanding of the need for flexible, responsive solutions. Even then, success remained an uphill battle. The path to educational equity felt like navigating a complex labyrinth, every step forward met with unforeseen obstacles, but we persisted, driven by the shared vision of a better future for all students.

The effort to improve educational equity was not without its challenges. Securing adequate funding remained a persistent obstacle, as competition for limited resources was intense. We encountered resistance from some community members and policymakers who questioned the need for increased spending on education or who prioritized other policy initiatives. Overcoming these challenges required building broad-based coalitions, educating the public about the importance of educational equity, and demonstrating the tangible benefits of investing in under-resourced schools.

Despite these challenges, our efforts yielded significant progress. We secured increased funding for schools in low-income areas, leading to improved school facilities, reduced class sizes, and increased access to educational resources. Our advocacy efforts resulted in policy changes that promoted teacher recruitment and retention, improved school climate, and enhanced parental engagement. The impact of these initiatives was evident in improved student achievement, higher graduation rates, and increased access to higher education opportunities for students in underserved communities.

The positive impact on the community was substantial. Improved educational outcomes led to enhanced economic opportunities for students, increased community stability, lowering crime rates, and a greater sense of hope for the future. The transformation of under-resourced schools into thriving learning environments fostered community pride and strengthened the social fabric of the Inland Empire. The success of these initiatives served as a powerful example of how a comprehensive approach to educational equity, combining advocacy, policy reform, community engagement, and direct school interventions, can achieve transformative change.

However, the work toward educational equity is far from complete. Ongoing economic disparities, coupled with the changing demographic landscape of the region, continue to pose significant challenges. The need for sustained investment in education, coupled with ongoing advocacy and community engagement, remains critical to ensuring that all students in the Inland Empire have equal access to a quality education and the opportunity to reach their full potential. The struggle for educational justice remains an integral part of the broader fight for a just and equitable society, and our commitment to this cause continues. The lessons learned underscore the importance of data-driven advocacy, collaborative partnerships, and unwavering dedication to the pursuit of educational justice for all. The journey towards equity demands constant vigilance, creative solutions, and a resilient commitment to creating a society where all children have the opportunity to thrive.

Our advocacy for policy change involved a multi-layered approach, recognizing that educational equity couldn't be achieved through isolated actions. We understood that systemic change required concerted efforts at the local, state, and national levels, engaging diverse stakeholders and employing various strategies to influence policy decisions. Our initial focus was on building strong relationships with local elected officials at multiple city halls and county supervisory offices throughout the region. This involved regular meetings, briefings on the educational disparities within our region, and collaborative efforts to identify potential solutions. We presented them with the data we had compiled – stark figures demonstrating the correlation between funding levels, school resources, and student achievement across various districts. This wasn't just about presenting statistics; it was about painting a human picture, sharing anecdotes of students struggling in dilapidated classrooms, teachers burdened by oversized classes, and parents desperately seeking ways to support their children's education.

These personal narratives, coupled with the hard data, proved incredibly effective in humanizing the issue and fostering empathy among policymakers. We found that personal stories resonated deeply with officials, often leading to more fruitful discussions and a greater willingness to support our proposed reforms. We worked closely with the local school board, attending meetings, presenting proposals, and actively participating in the development of the district's budget. We advocated for increased funding for specific programs, such as early childhood education, after-school programs, and professional development for teachers. This often involved negotiating compromises and building consensus among board members who held differing priorities.

Our lobbying efforts extended beyond the local level. We engaged in significant advocacy at the state level, working with state legislators to secure increased funding for education and to reform the state's funding formula. The state funding formula, at that time, was deeply flawed, disproportionately allocating resources to wealthier districts while leaving under-resourced communities struggling. We advocated for a more equitable formula that would ensure a fairer distribution of funds based on student needs, regardless of the district's property tax base. This involved extensive research, the development of detailed policy proposals, and numerous meetings with legislators and their staff. We developed a comprehensive policy brief outlining the need for change, supported by data and compelling case studies from the Inland Empire. We also organized meetings with key legislators, inviting parents, teachers, and students to share their personal experiences and underscore the urgency of the situation.

Building coalitions was paramount to our success. We worked with a diverse range of organizations, including teacher unions, parent advocacy groups, community organizations, and faith-based institutions. This broad-based coalition provided a powerful collective voice that resonated with policymakers. Together, we held press conferences, organized rallies, and launched public awareness campaigns to build public support for our policy proposals. These campaigns highlighted the negative consequences of educational inequity, emphasizing the long-term societal costs associated with under-resourced schools. We used social media effectively to raise awareness and mobilize public support.

We created compelling visuals and videos showcasing the realities of under-resourced schools, sharing student stories, and highlighting the positive impacts of our policy proposals.

Beyond lobbying and coalition-building, we focused significantly on public education and awareness campaigns. We organized town hall meetings, community forums, and educational workshops to engage the public and gain support for our cause. These forums provided opportunities to educate the community about the importance of educational equity, dispel misconceptions, and build consensus around our proposed policy changes.

We emphasized the link between education and economic opportunity, social mobility, and community well-being. We demonstrated how investing in education was not merely an expense but a strategic investment with significant long-term returns.

At the national level, we engaged with federal agencies and representatives to advocate for increased federal funding for education. While federal funding played a smaller role in our specific local context, advocating for increased national investment in education was crucial in ensuring a stable and equitable education system across the entire country. We understood that local and state efforts were often insufficient to address the deeply rooted systemic inequalities in education, necessitating a coordinated national approach. Our national advocacy involved attending national conferences, collaborating with national education organizations, and participating in policy debates on Capitol Hill. We focused on aligning our local advocacy with national policy initiatives, leveraging national support to amplify our efforts at the state and local levels.

Our advocacy efforts yielded tangible results. At the local level, we achieved significant increases in school funding, improvements in school infrastructure, and enhanced teacher training programs. At the state level, we secured revisions to the state funding formula, resulting in a more equitable distribution of resources across school districts. While we did not achieve all of our goals immediately, the progress made demonstrably improved the educational landscape within the Inland Empire. We successfully enacted legislation that mandated smaller class sizes in low-income schools, resulting in a more favorable teacher-student ratio and improved learning outcomes. We also secured funding for after-school programs and summer enrichment initiatives, providing students with extended learning opportunities outside of regular school hours.

However, the path to policy change was not without obstacles. We encountered resistance from some policymakers and community members who questioned the need for increased spending on education or who prioritized other policy initiatives. We also faced challenges in navigating the complex bureaucracy of national, state, and local government. These challenges required persistence, strategic planning, and strong coalition-building to overcome. We had to effectively counter arguments against increased education spending by demonstrating the long-term economic benefits of a well-educated workforce and a thriving community. We had to engage in painstaking negotiations, compromising where necessary while maintaining our core principles and objectives.

Ultimately, the success of our advocacy efforts stemmed from a combination of factors: strong data-driven research, compelling narratives, effective coalition-building, and persistent engagement with policymakers. Our commitment to building trust with communities, policymakers, and our organizational partners proved invaluable in creating sustainable change. It was a long, arduous process, requiring resilience, adaptability, and a deep commitment to educational justice. The journey highlighted the need for consistent advocacy, long-term planning, and ongoing evaluation of the impacts of implemented policies. The work continues, as the pursuit of educational equity remains an ongoing process requiring constant vigilance, creative solutions, and a steadfast commitment to ensuring that all children have the opportunity to thrive.

Building effective coalitions was not merely a strategic choice; it was the cornerstone of our success. We recognized that achieving systemic change in education required a unified front, a collective voice that transcended individual organizations and amplified the urgency of our cause. Our approach involved carefully identifying organizations and groups whose goals aligned with ours, and whose memberships could provide valuable resources and perspectives. This wasn't about simply adding numbers; it was about strategically assembling a diverse coalition capable of influencing policy and driving community-wide change.

One of our most crucial partnerships was with the Inland Empire's chapter of the California Teachers Association (CTA). Their membership comprised a vast network of educators possessing firsthand knowledge of the challenges faced in under-resourced schools. Their insights were invaluable in informing our policy proposals, providing realistic assessments of the feasibility of proposed changes, and offering practical strategies for implementation. Beyond their expertise, the CTA brought significant political clout to the table, enabling us to leverage their established relationships with state legislators and policymakers. Their endorsement provided much-needed credibility and legitimacy to our efforts, opening doors that might otherwise have remained closed.

We also forged strong alliances with several local parent advocacy groups. These groups represented the voices of parents directly affected by educational inequities, bringing a powerful emotional element to our advocacy efforts. Their personal stories of struggling children, navigating overcrowded classrooms, and lacking access to essential resources were incredibly persuasive in moving policymakers to action. These parents weren't simply statistics; they were the human face of the issue, vividly illustrating the real-world consequences of inadequate funding and systemic inequities. Their involvement strengthened our coalition, adding a critical element of authentic lived experience to our advocacy efforts.

Community-based organizations played a vital role in extending our reach and mobilizing support within the diverse communities of the Inland Empire. These groups, often rooted in specific neighborhoods and ethnic communities, possessed deep-seated knowledge of local needs and concerns, as well as established networks of trust and influence within their respective communities. By partnering with them, we were able to effectively disseminate information, garner local support for our proposals, and counter misinformation and resistance within specific communities. Their involvement was crucial in ensuring that our advocacy was not only effective but also culturally sensitive and responsive to the specific needs of all community members.

We also collaborated with several faith-based organizations, leveraging their established networks and moral authority to build support for our initiatives. Many faith communities are deeply invested in the well-being of their congregations and their children's education. By aligning our efforts with their shared values, we tapped into a powerful wellspring of community support. Their participation added a broader dimension to our advocacy efforts, highlighting the moral imperative of educational equity and attracting support from a wider cross-section of the community. Their involvement often extended beyond providing moral support; they frequently contributed volunteers to assist with outreach events, community forums, and voter registration drives.

The rationale for forming these partnerships was multifaceted. First and foremost, it was about maximizing our collective impact. By combining our resources and expertise, we were able to achieve far more than we could have individually. The combined influence of multiple organizations was far greater than the sum of their individual efforts. This synergy was critical in pushing for policy changes that would have been difficult, if not impossible, to achieve on our own.

Second, these partnerships provided access to critical resources. Each organization brought unique assets to the table, including funding, volunteers, communication networks, and political influence. These resources were essential in sustaining our long-term advocacy efforts. Pooling these resources allowed us to execute effectively broader campaigns, participate in more legislative processes, and sustain our community outreach programs.

Third, the partnerships built broader community support. A coalition of diverse organizations created a far more compelling and influential narrative than any single organization could have achieved on its own. This broad-based support created a powerful public pressure on policymakers to address educational inequities. It demonstrated a widespread commitment to improving the educational system, creating an environment where policymakers were more likely to listen and respond.

The impact of these collaborations extended far beyond securing immediate policy changes. They played a significant role in fostering community development and strengthening civic engagement. The process of working together fostered a sense of shared purpose and collective efficacy among community members. People from different backgrounds, with diverse perspectives and experiences, learned to work together towards a common goal. This collaboration generated a more cohesive and active citizenry, better equipped to address future community challenges.

The collaborative partnerships also had a significant impact on local governance. Our combined efforts increased the transparency and accountability of local school boards and government officials. The broad-based support for our advocacy initiatives created a more inclusive and responsive environment, where the voices of marginalized communities were heard and considered. This led to significant improvements in communication between the government and the community, resulting in greater civic participation and increased trust in public institutions.

The success we achieved in addressing educational inequities demonstrates the transformative power of building strong coalitions and partnerships. It wasn't about one organization or one individual; it was about the collective action of diverse groups working together with a shared vision and unwavering dedication. This collaborative approach not only secured policy changes that directly benefited students but also strengthened the community's ability to address future challenges and create lasting, positive change. The lessons learned from our collaborative efforts underscore the importance of collaboration, community engagement, and the transformative potential of collective action in advancing social justice. It's a model that can be replicated and adapted in other contexts, demonstrating the power of unity in achieving lasting social transformation. The ongoing work requires continued collaboration and a steadfast commitment to ensuring that all children have access to a quality education, regardless of their background or zip code.

The journey continues, with new challenges and opportunities arising each day, but the core principle remains the same: the power of collaborative action in the pursuit of social justice.

Chapter 4:

The Power of Ancestral Strength

My journey as an activist, educator, and community leader has been profoundly shaped by my heritage and the rich tapestry of my ancestors' lives. It is intertwined with the struggles and triumphs of marginalized communities, dating back to my grandparents' immigration from Mexico. Their journey led them to the fields of Southern California, where they toiled under the scorching sun, and later to the Sunkist Factory in Ontario, California. There, they faced relentless oppression and systemic racism, their brown skin a target for discrimination. This history is not merely a part of my background; it is intrinsic to my being, forming the foundation of my worldview and leadership style. It wasn't a conscious decision to leverage my background; rather, it was an inherent part of who I am, a foundation upon which my worldview and leadership style were built. Understanding my roots as Indigenous and Mexican-American, has been crucial in navigating the complexities of social justice work, providing me with a resilience and understanding that transcends mere intellectual comprehension.

Understanding my roots as Indigenous and Mexican-American has been pivotal in my navigation of social justice work. It has endowed me with resilience and an understanding that surpasses academic knowledge. I have witnessed firsthand the challenges faced by my community, and this has fueled my passion for creating change. My family's experiences have taught me the importance of resilience and the power of cultural heritage in overcoming adversity.

Their struggles were not isolated incidents; they represented a larger pattern of systemic oppression experienced by countless Mexican-Americans throughout history. Learning about their experiences – not just the broad strokes of history, but the intimate details of their daily lives, their hopes and fears, their triumphs and defeats – has shaped my understanding of the historical roots of current social injustices. This understanding, rooted in lived experience and intergenerational trauma, serves as a constant reminder of the gravity of my work and the urgency of creating lasting change. It's not just data points and statistics; it's the faces and stories of my ancestors staring back at me, urging me forward.

My journey and calling as an activist are deeply intertwined with the lives of my grandparents, who made the arduous journey from Mexico, leaving everything familiar behind. Among them was my grandmother, Guadalupe Nevarez, a strong and resilient woman whose daily rituals and deep connection with her heritage left an indelible mark on me.

Guadalupe's days began early, tending to her garden of herbs and nopales, an extension of her Indigenous roots. She believed in the healing powers of the earth and practiced traditional medicine, offering remedies to those in need. Her days were a blend of ancient traditions and quiet resilience as she cared for her family and navigated a new life in a foreign land. Her prayers and devotion to her faith were constant companions, the rosary a familiar comfort in a world that often showed her discrimination and hardship.

As a child, I would often accompany her in the garden, listening to stories of her life in Mexico and the challenges she faced as an immigrant. She instilled in me a sense of pride in our heritage and a deep understanding of the struggles faced by marginalized communities. Her strength and resilience in the face of adversity became my own, shaping my worldview and driving my passion for social justice.

My grandfather, Jose Nevarez, played an equally pivotal role in shaping my understanding of our heritage and its impact on my life path. He toiled in the vineyards and citrus groves, his hands calloused and stained from the labor of love that was providing for his family. The sun beat down on him relentlessly, but he persevered, his strength and determination mirroring that of the vibrant plants he nurtured. Later, he retired from the Sunkist Factory, but his work ethic and connection to the earth remained unwavering.

Each morning, I would wake to the familiar scent of fresh, homemade flour tortillas. Jose had risen early, as was his ritual, to prepare this staple of our heritage. The process was sacred to him, a communion of sorts, as he mixed, rolled, and cooked the tortillas with meticulous care. These mornings were a time for reflection and connection, a reminder of our roots and the importance of carrying on traditions.

As I partook in these morning rituals, I felt a sense of continuity with my heritage. Jose's stories of his days in the vineyards and his experiences as a Mexican-American worker mirrored the struggles of so many others. His resilience and pride in his culture, passed down through generations, empowered me to face the complexities of social justice work. It was through these daily rituals and the sharing of stories that I truly understood the impact of my heritage on my calling as an activist, educator, and community leader.

Beyond the immediate impact of my family's history, my cultural identity has significantly informed my approach to activism. The deep-rooted traditions of community support, mutual aid, and collective responsibility prevalent in many Mexican-American communities have shaped my understanding of effective community organizing. I learned to value consensus-building, collaboration, and empathy in my interactions with diverse groups of people. This approach reflects a profound understanding of the importance of inclusivity in achieving lasting social change. Building consensus is not merely a political strategy; it is a testament to a deeply held belief in the power of unity and a profound respect for diverse perspectives stemming from my cultural roots and understandings of community before self.

The strength and resilience of my ancestors, forged in their struggles, have been my beacon in the often disheartening world of social justice work. Their stories of resistance and perseverance against systemic racism and oppression are not unique, but they are deeply personal. Understanding the broader history of Indigenous suffering and resistance in the face of colonizing forces has given me a deeper appreciation for the strength of my community.

The values of mutual aid and collective responsibility, so integral to Mexican-American communities, are a testament to our resilience and a powerful tool for activism. This sense of community, built on a foundation of shared struggles and support, has been a guiding light in my journey. It has taught me that true leadership lies in understanding the interconnectedness of our experiences and the power of unity.

The stories of my grandparents, Guadalupe and Jose Nevarez, embody this interconnectedness. Their daily rituals, steeped in our Indigenous and Mexican heritage, were a form of resistance against the discrimination they faced. Guadalupe's connection to the earth and her practice of traditional medicine were extensions of her Indigenous roots, a quiet rebellion against the oppression faced by her community. Jose's unwavering work ethic and pride in providing for his family mirrored the resilience of the vibrant plants he nurtured. Their struggles and strengths were my inheritance, shaping my worldview and fueling my passion for social justice. Their experiences taught me the importance of perseverance, the need to maintain hope in the face of adversity, and the value of finding strength in collective action. The historical narrative wasn't just about overcoming hardship; it was about learning from it, about understanding that progress is rarely linear, and that setbacks are inevitable parts of a larger transformative journey. The importance of enduring, persistent effort became deeply ingrained, an understanding fueled by the legacy of past generations.

Moreover, the ancestral wisdom passed down through generations has provided me with a framework for understanding the complexities of systemic oppression and the importance of creating transformative change. This wisdom, passed down through storytelling, oral traditions, and cultural practices, serves as a potent counter-narrative to the dominant narratives that often marginalize and silence the voices of marginalized communities. This counter-narrative is not merely an alternative perspective; it is a crucial corrective to the incomplete, often distorted, historical accounts that have long been pervasive.

My ancestral strength is not merely a historical legacy; it is a living force that continues to shape my work today. It is a reminder of the profound resilience and unwavering spirit of my Indigenous ancestors, and a constant source of inspiration and guidance as I navigate the complexities of my work. It underscores the profound connection between personal history and public service, a connection that serves as a constant reminder of the critical importance of intergenerational collaboration and the enduring impact of past struggles on current social justice efforts. This deeply ingrained understanding shapes my approach, fueling my resilience and inspiring my commitment to creating a more just and equitable future for all. The ongoing work is a testament to this enduring heritage and a commitment to honoring the legacy of past generations. The struggles of the past fuel the efforts of the present, ensuring that future generations will benefit from the legacy of collective action and unwavering dedication.

The strength I draw from my ancestors isn't solely individual resilience; it's deeply intertwined with the vibrant, enduring power of community traditions. My family's history, like that of many Mexican-American families, is a testament to the unwavering support systems forged within our communities. These weren't merely social gatherings; they were lifelines, offering mutual aid, collective action, and a shared sense of purpose that transcended personal hardship. The strength found in collective action, in the shared burden and shared joy, is a legacy passed down through generations, shaping my understanding of effective social change.

This understanding, rooted in my Mexican-American heritage, takes on a deeper dimension when explored through the lens of oral traditions. The stories shared within my community were not simply a means of entertainment, but powerful instruments of knowledge transmission and empathy-building. They served as a vessel for preserving history, ensuring that the emotional weight of lived experiences was felt across generations.

During family gatherings and church events, I listened intently as elders recounted the struggles and triumphs of our ancestors. These narratives were dynamic, evolving to adapt to the changing present while retaining the core values that defined us—community and perseverance. Among these stories were the legends of the Hopi, detailing the forward walk of their people and the birth, destruction, and rebirth of their five worlds. The legacy of the Kachina and their reverence for Tawa, the sun god, wove a spiritual thread through our history, connecting us to the divine and the ancestral.

The oral tradition allowed me to absorb the emotional resonance of social justice battles, both past and present. It instilled in me a profound respect for the power of collective action and mutual aid. These stories were our strength, a reminder that we are part of something greater than ourselves and that our individual struggles are intertwined with the enduring power of community traditions.

Beyond storytelling, the significance of community gatherings cannot be overstated. These weren't simply occasions for socializing; they were vital mechanisms for information sharing, resource mobilization, and collective decision-making. Church services, community meetings, and family reunions provided platforms for organizing, strategizing, and supporting one another. In times of crisis – be it economic hardship, natural disasters, or acts of injustice – these gatherings became hubs of resilience, where resources were pooled, skills were shared, and a collective spirit of determination was nurtured. This collective spirit wasn't abstract; it manifested in tangible ways, such as communal childcare, shared meals, and coordinated efforts to address community needs for field workers facing homelessness. The sense of unity and belonging fostered within these gatherings was paramount to survival and empowered us to face challenges that would have been insurmountable alone. This collective strength is a model of effective community organization, a testament to the power of human connection in the face of adversity.

The role of cultural events in maintaining community unity and mobilizing support is equally significant. From Mariachi music, to Aztec drum circles and traditional Aztec dances, these events served as powerful expressions of cultural identity, providing a space for celebrating heritage and reaffirming shared values. These weren't merely performances; they were acts of resistance, preserving cultural traditions in the face of oppression and offering solace and affirmation. The music, the dance, the shared experience – all contributed to a sense of community and instilled a profound sense of cultural pride, strengthening our resolve and bolstering our sense of self-worth. It was through these events that we reinforced our bonds, shared our stories, and maintained our cultural heritage. This active preservation was a form of resistance, keeping our history alive and ensuring future generations would benefit from this rich cultural legacy. The cultural continuity itself became a powerful symbol of resilience and a source of strength, reminding us of our shared history and our collective power.

The methods employed for increasing participation in community initiatives were often innovative and highly effective. The reliance on word-of-mouth, informal networks, and personal connections ensured broad reach and fostered a sense of ownership within the community. Trust was paramount; decisions were made collaboratively, reflecting a deep understanding of the importance of consensus-building. The leaders emerged organically, often reflecting the community's diverse needs and experiences. These weren't hierarchical structures but collaborative networks, valuing the input and contributions of each individual member. This participatory approach ensured that initiatives were relevant, sustainable, and truly reflected the needs and aspirations of the community. The success of these community-led initiatives demonstrated the potential of empowering local communities to shape their own destiny.

The community's approach to conflict resolution was also notable. Mediation, negotiation, and reconciliation were prioritized over confrontation. Disputes were addressed within the community, often through informal processes that emphasized dialogue, understanding, and restorative justice. This approach fostered a strong sense of social cohesion and minimized the potential for conflict to escalate. It is important to note that while these were primarily informal methods, they often proved more effective than formal systems in addressing community conflicts, demonstrating the strength of community-based conflict resolution. This process prioritized healing and reconciliation, reflecting a deep-seated belief in the importance of unity and preserving communal harmony.

Furthermore, the role of faith-based organizations in community life was central. Churches served not only as places of worship but as crucial centers for social support, mutual aid, and community organizing. They provided food, shelter, and other essential resources to those in need, and they offered a safe and supportive environment for individuals and families facing hardship. These institutions fostered a strong sense of community and played a significant role in maintaining social cohesion and providing stability during times of adversity. They acted as a safety net, offering support, guidance, and a sense of belonging that extended far beyond religious doctrine. Their role was multifaceted, encompassing both spiritual and practical aspects of community life.

Looking back, I recognize that the strength of my ancestors wasn't merely a matter of individual fortitude; it was the collective strength of a community working together, sharing resources, supporting each other, and fighting for a better future. The rich tapestry of traditions, the collective wisdom passed down through generations, and the enduring power of community support all contributed to a resilience that transcended individual hardship and fueled a relentless pursuit of justice. This legacy serves as a constant source of inspiration and guidance, shaping my understanding of leadership, activism, and the pursuit of a more equitable society. The lessons learned within the heart of my community continue to inform my work today. The collective strength, the commitment to community, and the enduring power of tradition remain vital tools in the ongoing fight for social justice. This legacy of collective action, of unwavering support, and of enduring faith in the power of community, serves as the bedrock upon which I continue to build my efforts for a more just and equitable world. The strength of my heritage isn't just a historical narrative; it is a living, breathing testament to the enduring power of community and the transformative potential of collective action. It is a testament to the profound interconnectedness of personal history and public service, a connection that guides my every step and fuels my unwavering commitment to creating a more just future for all. The ongoing struggle for social justice finds its sustenance in the strength of these traditions, a legacy that I am committed to preserving and honoring.

The enduring strength derived from my ancestors isn't solely a product of individual resilience; it's fundamentally rooted in the intricate web of intergenerational collaboration and mentorship that has sustained our community across decades. This isn't merely a passing of the torch, but a dynamic exchange, a continuous conversation across generations, enriching and strengthening the collective movement for social justice. The wisdom, strategies, and unwavering commitment of older generations provide a crucial foundation upon which younger activists build, adapting and innovating while preserving the core values that have fueled our progress for generations.

This intergenerational connection is more than a symbolic gesture; it's a pragmatic necessity. The lived experiences of older generations, marked by the struggles and triumphs of the Chicano Civil Rights Movement and beyond, provide invaluable context and perspective for younger activists navigating the complexities of contemporary social justice battles. Their understanding of systemic oppression, their knowledge of historical precedents, and their honed skills in strategic organizing are irreplaceable assets. These aren't simply historical anecdotes; they are crucial lessons in navigating power structures, understanding the nuances of resistance, and maintaining resilience in the face of setbacks.

For example, I recall countless conversations with community elders who participated in the Brown Berets, the sit-ins, and the voter registration drives of the 1960s. Their stories weren't just tales of historical events; they were masterclasses in nonviolent resistance, community organizing, and the enduring power of collective action. They described the challenges, the sacrifices, and the overwhelming sense of shared purpose that bound them together during those turbulent times. Their experiences provided crucial context for understanding the systemic barriers that persist today and for developing effective strategies for dismantling them. These were not merely historical accounts; they were blueprints for future action.

The mentorship offered by these seasoned activists from the Brown Berets and the League of United Latin American Citizens (LULAC) extends beyond historical recounting; it involves the direct transmission of practical skills and strategies. They shared their knowledge of grassroots organizing, coalition-building, and effective communication—skills honed over decades of activism. They taught the importance of building trust within communities, the power of storytelling, and the necessity of persistent advocacy, even when I disagreed with their old ways of organizing. This hands-on mentorship, this direct transfer of experience, is invaluable in developing a new generation of leaders capable of sustaining the movement.

This intergenerational collaboration is not a one-way street. Younger activists bring their own unique perspectives, skills, and technologies to the table. Their fluency in digital communication, their understanding of social media activism, and their innovative approaches to community engagement contribute significantly to the movement's evolution. They challenge traditional approaches, introduce new strategies, and broaden the movement's reach and impact. They bring fresh energy, creativity, and a deep understanding of contemporary challenges. This dynamic interplay between experience and innovation is critical for ensuring the movement's adaptability and long-term sustainability.

The establishment of formal mentorship programs within our community has further solidified this intergenerational partnership. These programs facilitate structured relationships between younger and older activists, providing opportunities for shared learning, skill development, and the building of enduring bonds. These programs aren't simply about imparting knowledge; they're about fostering relationships, building trust, and creating a sense of shared purpose across generations. They create a supportive environment where mentees can openly discuss challenges, learn from mistakes, and receive the guidance they need to succeed.

One such program, "Operation Daybreak," pairs seasoned activists with young leaders looking to join a prestigious military academy, offering a structured framework for mentorship. The initiative includes workshops, seminars, and individual mentoring sessions focused on leadership development, strategic planning, test taking, maintaining high academic achievement standards and community engagement. The results have been remarkable, with young leaders demonstrating increased confidence, enhanced organizational skills, and a deepened commitment to social justice being accepted into military academies in 2025 and beyond. This program serves as a model for creating sustainable intergenerational partnerships, ensuring the continuity of the movement and the development of future leaders at tables where we lack representation.

However, the success of intergenerational collaboration isn't solely dependent on formal structures. It requires a conscious effort to cultivate relationships, to bridge generational gaps, and to foster mutual respect and understanding. This involves creating inclusive spaces where individuals from different age groups can share their perspectives, learn from one another, and work collaboratively toward shared goals. This necessitates active listening, open communication, and a willingness to embrace diverse perspectives. It means recognizing the strengths and contributions of each generation and creating opportunities for them to complement and enhance one another.

The challenges involved in intergenerational collaboration should not be overlooked. Different generations may have varying communication styles, differing approaches to problem-solving, and even differing views on the best way to achieve social justice. Navigating these differences requires patience, understanding, and a commitment to building bridges. This is a continuous process, requiring ongoing dialogue and a willingness to adapt and compromise. However, overcoming these challenges is crucial for ensuring the effectiveness and sustainability of the movement. The rewards, however, far outweigh the challenges.

The transfer of knowledge and skills across generations is also crucial in ensuring the continuation of the movement. This involves not just the sharing of tactical information, but also the transmission of values, principles, and the historical context that shapes our struggle. This includes passing down the stories of resistance, the lessons learned from past struggles, and the enduring hope that fuels our pursuit of justice. The sharing of oral histories, the preservation of archives, and the creation of educational materials are essential elements of this transmission process.

Furthermore, intergenerational collaboration strengthens leadership development within the community. Mentorship provides young leaders with invaluable guidance, support, and the opportunity to learn from the experiences of those who have come before them. This process fosters a sense of continuity, ensuring that the movement's values and goals are carried forward to future generations. It empowers young leaders to assume positions of responsibility, shaping the direction of the movement and ensuring its continued relevance.

Beyond formal programs, informal mentoring relationships play a vital role in this intergenerational exchange. These spontaneous interactions, occurring during community events, workshops, and casual conversations, provide opportunities for the transfer of knowledge and experience in a more organic and less structured setting. These less formal relationships often form the backbone of intergenerational collaboration, building strong bonds and fostering a sense of shared commitment.

In conclusion, the power of ancestral strength is deeply intertwined with the dynamic exchange between generations.

Intergenerational collaboration and mentorship are not merely desirable attributes; they are fundamental to the sustainability and success of the movement for social justice. The continued success of our struggle hinges upon the ability of older and younger generations to work together, learn from one another, and pass the torch of activism to future generations, carrying with it the wisdom, resilience, and unwavering commitment that has defined our journey for decades. This continuous dialogue, this symbiotic relationship, is the very lifeblood of our movement, ensuring its strength and longevity in the pursuit of a just and equitable society. The legacy of struggle, resilience, and unwavering hope—this is the true power of ancestral strength, a force amplified and sustained by the ongoing conversation between generations.

The strength we draw from our ancestors, as discussed previously, is not simply a linear inheritance; it's a vibrant tapestry woven from the threads of countless individual experiences, each contributing uniquely to the rich texture of our collective struggle. This understanding must encompass the profound contributions of individuals from diverse cultural backgrounds, whose experiences have shaped the strategies, goals, and very essence of the environmental justice movement. Ignoring or marginalizing these voices would be a profound disservice to the movement's vitality and potential. Celebrating cultural diversity is not merely a matter of political correctness; it's a fundamental necessity for building a truly effective and inclusive movement capable of addressing the complex environmental challenges we face.

The environmental justice movement, at its core, tackles issues deeply intertwined with social and economic inequalities. These inequalities often intersect with and exacerbate existing disparities based on race, ethnicity, class, gender, and geographic location. Recognizing this multifaceted nature of environmental injustice necessitates a diverse movement capable of understanding and responding to the specific needs and concerns of various communities. A movement composed primarily of one demographic group would inevitably lack the breadth of experience and perspective necessary to effectively advocate for the broadest possible range of affected populations.

For instance, Indigenous communities across the globe have for centuries possessed a deep, interconnected understanding of the environment and its vital role in their cultures and livelihoods. Their traditional ecological knowledge (TEK), honed through generations of observation and practice, provides invaluable insights into sustainable resource management, biodiversity conservation, and the interconnectedness of ecological systems. Ignoring this invaluable knowledge base would be akin to discarding a crucial tool in the fight for environmental justice. Their struggles against resource extraction, land dispossession, and environmental degradation represent a long and often brutal history, offering critical lessons for contemporary environmental activism. The wisdom and resilience of these communities are vital components of the broader movement.

Similarly, communities of color, particularly in urban environments, often bear the brunt of environmental hazards, from polluted air and water to toxic waste sites. These communities, burdened by historical and systemic injustices, frequently lack the resources and political power to effectively address these environmental threats. Their lived experiences—the firsthand accounts of environmental racism and its devastating consequences—provide crucial evidence and fuel the movement's fight for environmental equity. Their stories, often unheard or dismissed, hold the key to crafting impactful narratives capable of swaying public opinion and inspiring action.

The contributions of women to the environmental justice movement are equally profound, yet often remain underrecognized. Women, across diverse cultures and communities, play critical roles in environmental stewardship, from managing household resources to actively participating in community-based conservation efforts. Their unique perspectives, often grounded in their roles within their families and communities, offer a distinct lens through which to understand the interconnectedness of environmental and social issues. Their participation in leadership roles within the movement is not merely a matter of fairness; it's a crucial element in ensuring that the movement's strategies and goals reflect the diverse needs and perspectives of its constituents.

Furthermore, the inclusion of individuals with disabilities within the movement enriches its understanding of environmental accessibility and inclusivity. Their lived experiences highlight the critical need to address environmental barriers that limit access to natural spaces and environmental resources for people with disabilities.

Their insights are vital in shaping policies and practices that promote universal design and environmental justice for all members of society.

The power of diverse perspectives lies not only in their unique contributions but also in their potential for collaborative synergy. When individuals from different backgrounds, with their varied experiences and understandings, come together, they generate a dynamic exchange of ideas, approaches, and strategies. This synergistic effect fosters innovation, enhances problem-solving capabilities, and ultimately strengthens the movement's overall effectiveness.

The celebration of cultural diversity within the environmental justice movement extends beyond simple representation; it requires a conscious effort to create truly inclusive spaces where individuals from all backgrounds feel valued, respected, and empowered to participate fully. This includes addressing issues of language barriers, cultural sensitivity, and power imbalances within the movement's structure. Building trust and fostering open communication are critical for ensuring that all voices are heard and valued.

Creating opportunities for cross-cultural exchange and collaboration is essential. This can involve organizing workshops, conferences, and other events that bring together individuals from diverse backgrounds. It also requires promoting intercultural understanding and communication skills among movement members. The goal is to create a movement that actively embraces and celebrates its diversity as a source of strength and innovation.

The concept of "intersectional environmentalism" reflects this emphasis on understanding the interconnectedness of various social and environmental issues. It recognizes that environmental problems are often inextricably linked to issues of race, class, gender, and other forms of social inequality. By embracing an intersectional approach, the movement can more effectively address the root causes of environmental injustice and create solutions that promote equity and sustainability for all.

The adoption of culturally sensitive communication strategies is crucial. This includes adapting messaging and outreach efforts to resonate with specific communities, taking into account language, cultural norms, and communication styles. It also involves recognizing and respecting diverse worldviews and perspectives on environmental issues. The movement must be aware of and sensitive to the varied ways in which people relate to and interact with their environment.

Furthermore, the movement should strive to build relationships and partnerships with community-based organizations and grassroots groups that represent the interests of diverse communities. Collaboration with these groups not only ensures that the movement's strategies and actions are responsive to the specific needs of various communities but also strengthens the movement's grassroots base and amplifies its reach.

The celebration of cultural diversity is not just a matter of representation; it's a vital strategy for building a powerful and effective environmental justice movement. By embracing and celebrating its diversity, the movement can enhance its capacity for innovation, broaden its base of support, and strengthen its ability to address the complex challenges of environmental injustice. This requires ongoing commitment to inclusivity, intercultural understanding, and the recognition of the profound contributions of individuals from all backgrounds. Only then can the environmental justice movement achieve its ultimate goal: a world where environmental sustainability and social justice are inextricably linked and enjoyed by all.

The enduring strength of the communities engaged in the fight for environmental justice in the Inland Empire and beyond lies not just in their immediate victories but in the lasting impact of their collective action. Their struggles have woven a rich tapestry of resilience, demonstrating the transformative power of community solidarity in the face of overwhelming odds. The legacy of their activism extends far beyond specific legislative wins or court decisions; it's embedded in the strengthened bonds between neighbors, the increased political awareness, and the enduring commitment to environmental stewardship that permeates the region. These communities have not only fought for clean air and water, but they have also built strong, resilient networks capable of facing future environmental challenges.

One of the most significant legacies of these movements is the development of sophisticated organizing models and strategies. Years of experience battling powerful corporations and unsympathetic government agencies have honed the skills of community activists. They have learned how to effectively mobilize their constituents, conduct thorough research of environmental impact reports and city general plans, frame their arguments persuasively, and negotiate with

decision-makers. This accumulated knowledge forms a valuable resource, not only for the Inland Empire but also for environmental justice movements across the country and globally. The strategies developed and refined in these local battles—such as using citizen science to gather data, employing effective media strategies to amplify their voices through press releases, and building powerful coalitions with diverse stakeholders—provide replicable models for future activism. These are not merely theoretical frameworks but battle-tested methods, honed in the crucible of real-world struggle.

Furthermore, these communities have demonstrated the profound importance of long-term commitment and perseverance. The fight for environmental justice is rarely a quick victory; it often involves protracted legal battles, arduous organizing efforts, and consistent engagement over many years. The unwavering dedication of these communities, their ability to sustain their momentum through setbacks and disappointments, serves as a potent lesson in the power of sustained collective action. Their persistence demonstrates that progress, while sometimes incremental, is ultimately possible through persistent engagement and unwavering belief in the cause. This enduring commitment is a vital element of their enduring legacy, serving as an inspiration for future generations of activists.

The collective action undertaken by these communities has had a profound impact on the political landscape of the Inland Empire. They have successfully influenced local, state, and even national policy, pushing for stricter environmental regulations, increased funding for environmental remediation projects, and greater community involvement in environmental decision-making. Their persistent advocacy has shifted the political discourse, making environmental issues a priority for elected officials and increasing the public's awareness of environmental injustices. This increased political engagement extends beyond environmental concerns, empowering communities to advocate for a wider range of social justice issues, strengthening their overall political voice and capacity.

Beyond the tangible achievements, the enduring legacy of these communities rests on the intangible yet powerful bonds of community solidarity that have been forged in the process. The shared experiences of struggle, the collective victories, and the mutual support offered in times of difficulty have strengthened community ties, creating a resilient social fabric capable of weathering future storms. This strong sense of community is not simply a byproduct of the activism; it is a critical component of its success. It demonstrates the power of collective action to build stronger, more cohesive communities. The relationships built through shared struggle are a vital part of the movement's enduring power. These bonds extend beyond the immediate activist network, shaping the cultural landscape and social interactions within the broader community.

Moreover, the legacy of these communities extends to the invaluable lessons learned about the intersectionality of environmental justice and social justice. The communities involved have often faced multiple forms of marginalization—based on race, class, ethnicity, and other factors—highlighting the intricate connection between environmental degradation and broader social inequities. Their experiences have brought to light the disproportionate impact of environmental hazards on vulnerable populations, emphasizing the need for policies that address both environmental and social justice concerns simultaneously. This integrated approach to problem-solving forms a crucial part of their lasting contribution, underscoring the inseparability of environmental and social equity.

The impact of their activism is not limited to the Inland Empire; it resonates across geographical boundaries and inspires environmental justice movements nationally and internationally. Their victories, strategies, and lessons learned provide a blueprint for communities facing similar challenges, demonstrating the power of collective action, perseverance, and community solidarity in the fight for environmental justice. The dissemination of knowledge and experience through networks of activists, publications, and conferences strengthens and emboldens movements in other areas facing similar environmental threats. This sharing of experience fosters cross-pollination of ideas and strategies, ultimately expanding the reach and effectiveness of the environmental justice movement.

The continuing need for environmental justice in the Inland Empire and beyond underscores the enduring relevance of these communities' legacy. While significant progress has been made, numerous environmental challenges persist, necessitating ongoing advocacy, vigilance, and community engagement. The work is far from finished; new threats emerge, and ongoing challenges persist. The legacy of past activism provides a crucial foundation for future action, highlighting the need for sustained commitment, effective strategies, and strong community solidarity. The fight continues, building upon the groundwork laid by those who have come before, inspiring future generations to carry on the torch.

In conclusion, the enduring legacy of these communities transcends specific legislative victories or short-term accomplishments. It is deeply rooted in the empowerment of communities, the development of effective organizing strategies, the strengthening of social bonds, the increased political awareness, and the ongoing commitment to environmental justice. Their resilience, perseverance, and unwavering dedication serve as a powerful testament to the transformative power of collective action and the enduring importance of community solidarity in the ongoing fight for a just and sustainable future for all. This legacy is a source of inspiration and a roadmap for future generations of activists working to achieve environmental justice, not only in the Inland Empire but across the globe. The fight for environmental justice is a marathon, not a sprint, and the enduring strength of these communities serves as a powerful reminder of the importance of long-term commitment, strategic planning, commitment to voting, and unwavering solidarity in the pursuit of a healthier and more equitable world.

Chapter 5:

From Grassroots to Congress

The culmination of years spent organizing within the Inland Empire's environmental justice movement brought a profound realization for me: the limitations of grassroots activism alone. While community organizing had yielded significant victories – forcing polluters to account for their actions, raising public awareness, and influencing local policy decisions – systemic change required a different approach. The deeply ingrained inequalities perpetuated by existing power structures demanded a more direct engagement with the levers of power. This realization led our coalition to a decision that would profoundly alter the course of my life and impact on the fight for environmental justice: I would enter the political arena.

The transition wasn't easy. The world of politics, with its intricate rules, complex negotiations, and often cynical machinations, presented a stark contrast to the passionate, community-focused work I had known. The clear-cut morality of fighting against corporate polluters blurred into the gray areas of political compromise and strategic maneuvering. Winning hearts and minds in a community was one thing; navigating the labyrinthine corridors of power, dealing with political maneuvering and compromise, was an entirely different challenge.

Initially, the idea felt overwhelming. The thought of running for office conjured images of relentless fundraising, contentious debates, and the relentless scrutiny of the media and opponents. The very notion of campaigning, of asking for votes, felt alien to someone who had always focused on empowering communities rather than seeking personal recognition. Doubt gnawed at my core, fueled by the anxieties of stepping outside my comfort zone into the unfamiliar and often unforgiving world of formal politics.

Yet, the weight of the environmental injustices I had witnessed, the countless stories of families suffering from polluted air and water, spurred me forward. The persistent battles against powerful corporations and indifferent government agencies had instilled in me an unwavering determination. Recognizing that while community organizing remained crucial, achieving lasting, systemic change required working within the political system, influencing legislation, and shaping policies at a higher level.

My decision was not made lightly. It involved extensive discussions with fellow activists, community members, and mentors who had navigated the complexities of political engagement. I sought their guidance, their wisdom, and their support, recognizing the need for a robust network to guide me through this new terrain. These conversations were instrumental in shaping my strategy and reinforcing my determination. They helped me understand the nuances of political strategy, the importance of coalition building, and the need to adapt my communication style to resonate with a broader audience.

The first step was building a strong campaign team. Assembling a diverse group of individuals— seasoned political strategists, experienced community organizers, passionate young volunteers, and trusted friends – each bringing their unique skills and perspectives to the table. This team became my bedrock, providing unwavering support and invaluable guidance throughout the grueling campaign process. They managed my schedule, crafted our team's message, organized fundraising events, and mobilized volunteers. The diverse composition of the team, reflective of the community it served, was crucial in ensuring a campaign that resonated authentically with diverse groups of voters.

Fundraising, a critical aspect of any political campaign, proved to be a significant hurdle. Unlike well-funded corporate interests, my campaign relied heavily on grassroots support from fellow community members. We organized numerous community events, focusing on transparent communication and highlighting our commitment to the community. We explained how our work in the environmental justice movement directly addressed the concerns of the people who lived, worked, and raised families in our community. This approach, grounded in honesty and relatability, resonated with a wide base of supporters, who contributed their time, skills, and resources. The success of the fundraising effort underscored the power of community solidarity, demonstrating that a grassroots campaign could compete effectively with better-funded opponents, with my campaign receiving 7,000 votes for $15,000.00 while my opponents received 8,000 votes for $300,000.00.

The campaign itself was an intensive period of intense engagement. My team and I traveled tirelessly, attending town hall meetings, knocking on doors, and participating in debates.

We learned to articulate our vision for the community in concise, persuasive language, adapting our message to resonate with diverse audiences. My background in community organizing provided an invaluable foundation, giving me the ability to connect with voters on a personal level and build trust. The relentless schedule demanded sacrifice, testing resilience and determination. The support of my family, friends, and campaign team became essential in sustaining me through this challenging period.

The election itself was a nail-biting affair, a testament to the power of community organizing and grassroots activism. The campaign's message— rooted in environmental justice, community empowerment, and collaborative governance— resonated with voters tired of partisan gridlock and disconnected politicians. The success of the campaign demonstrated that a candidate committed to addressing the concerns of everyday citizens could effectively compete in a crowded political landscape by uniting the people across party lines over issues that brought people together. It showcased the power of community-based political strategies, demonstrating that community members in any region could have an immense impact on the political process by taking time to get to know the candidates, the issues, and important election dates.

My victory in bringing people together was not simply a personal triumph; it marked a significant shift in the political landscape of the Inland Empire. It symbolized the empowerment of grassroots movements and the potential for community activists to become effective political leaders. This experience highlighted a pathway for others to bridge the gap between community activism and formal politics, demonstrating that the skills honed in the crucible of community organizing were directly transferable to the world of electoral politics.

Entering the political arena presented a steep learning curve. My team and I had to navigate the intricacies of legislative processes, master the art of political negotiation, and learn how to work effectively with diverse political actors, some of whom held views that conflicted starkly with my own. We adapted our strategies, learning to leverage my background in grassroots organizing while becoming proficient in the language and strategies of formal politics.

The transition from grassroots activist to political candidate was not without its challenges. I faced pressure to compromise on my principles, to dilute my message, and to engage in the political gamesmanship that often characterized formal politics. But I remained true to my core values, committed to the principles I was raised with as a Mexican-American, and unyielding in my commitment to environmental justice as a science teacher. I found ways to navigate these complexities without compromising my integrity, consistently seeking strategies to achieve goals while staying true to the values that defined me.

Over time, I found my effectiveness on the political campaign trail growing. I skillfully built coalitions, reaching out to like-minded individuals across the political spectrum and working hand-in-hand with them to achieve our shared goals. I used my knowledge of community dynamics to build consensus and foster collaboration. My success wasn't just about individual talent; it was a direct result of my commitment to inclusive governance across various industries and my ability to effectively engage diverse stakeholders. I felt a deep satisfaction in bringing people together and making a real difference.

Furthermore, I leveraged my position to amplify the voices of marginalized communities, ensuring that their concerns were heard and addressed within the political process - becoming a powerful advocate for policies that addressed the root causes of environmental injustice, working tirelessly to advance legislation that promoted environmental equity and social justice. I used my position to push for environmental protection measures that safeguarded the health of communities and the environment, pushing forward on issues that had been sidelined for years.

My journey underscores the crucial role that community activists can play in shaping the political landscape. It demonstrates the importance of bringing grassroots experience and perspectives into formal politics to create a more representative and responsive government and serves as an inspiration and a guide for those seeking to transition from activism to political leadership, showing that the principles of community organizing and empowerment can be effectively translated into success.

The enduring legacy of my journey extends far beyond my individual achievements. It represents the power of community organizing to foster genuine political change. It illustrates how grassroots activism can be a powerful catalyst for societal transformation and how individuals committed to social justice can make a profound impact by actively participating in the political process. My story becomes a source of inspiration, a testament to the enduring power of community mobilization, and a reminder that the fight for environmental justice extends beyond the streets and into the halls of power. My continued engagement in politics ensures a lasting legacy and serves as an example for future generations of activists striving to make a difference.

Navigating the intricacies of the campaign trail proved to be a significant undertaking for me. The transition from the relatively straightforward morality of grassroots activism to the nuanced world of compromise and strategic maneuvering required a considerable shift in perspective and approach. While the passion and dedication that fueled my activism remained constant, I had to learn to operate within a system that often prioritized expediency and negotiation over unwavering principle.

The transition from grassroots activism to the world of politics was a daunting one. I had always been passionate about social justice and creating change, but I soon realized that the political system was a complex web of compromise and strategy. While my dedication to my beliefs remained unwavering, I understood that I had to adapt my approach if I wanted to make a lasting impact. The decision to run for Congress was not made lightly. I had witnessed the power of grassroots movements and the impact we could have on the ground, but it wasn't enough.

I didn't run because I wanted power. I ran because I was tired of asking permission to breathe, to live, and to make decisions about our health and our future. I was tired of seeing the people I cared about being ignored and their needs sidelined. The halls of power were making decisions that affected our lives, and yet, they remained distant and disconnected from the very people they claimed to serve. The evictions, the polluted air, the broken promises—they all weighed heavily on me. I knew that we needed a voice, someone who understood the struggles and could navigate the political maze with our best interests at heart.

So, I took a deep breath and decided to run, knowing full well the ramifications. I ran, knowing that it would be a challenging journey, but one that was necessary. I had to learn quickly, adapting my ideals and principles to a world of negotiation and compromise. It was a tightrope walk, balancing my unwavering beliefs with the expediency often required on the campaign. But I remained focused, knowing that the reason I ran was bigger than any challenge I faced.

Building consensus proved to be a significant challenge. My commitment to environmental justice often clashed with the conflicting interests of powerful lobbies and entrenched political ideologies. I had to learn the art of negotiation, compromise, and persuasion, finding common ground with individuals who initially held opposing viewpoints. This required a level of political acumen that transcended my previous experience in community organizing. I discovered that building bridges required patience, empathy, and a willingness to listen and understand diverse perspectives. I found myself wrestling with the complexities of each negotiation, often feeling the weight of responsibility for finding a solution that satisfied everyone, a near impossible task. I learned to value every small victory, every grudging concession, as a step forward. It was exhausting, exhilarating, and ultimately, deeply rewarding to witness the power of collaboration.

The influence of money in politics was another significant hurdle I had to navigate. My grassroots campaign had shown me the power of community mobilization and fundraising, but the sheer scale of money wielded by the established players was terrifying. I learned to leverage my strong community ties to build support for my legislative initiatives, rallying constituents myself, urging them to contact their representatives and advocate for my policies. I also mastered the art of securing endorsements, working tirelessly to gain the support of influential figures and organizations. Their backing was crucial; it amplified my message and lent me much-needed credibility.

The media was a constant presence, shaping how people saw me and influencing the entire campaign. I learned to work with the press strategically, carefully crafting my messages to connect with different news outlets and their audiences. I knew how powerful effective communication could be – it shaped public opinion and steered the course of the campaign. I became a skilled communicator, able to explain complex issues clearly and persuasively. I used my understanding of the community to tailor my message, making sure it landed right.

I didn't hire political strategists from D.C. I built my team the way I build community: with trust. I surrounded myself with teachers, young climate activists, artists, grandmothers – even first-generation college students who, I'll never forget, translated city documents and designed our flyers. We brought together people who'd long been ignored by politics, and I told them, directly, "This campaign is yours too." Hearing Sofia, a campaign volunteer from Chaffey College, say, "I'd never seen someone who looked like my mom running for office. Then I met *me*, and suddenly I saw myself too," – that's what it was all about. We met in living rooms and cafés, just like I'd always done. I remember the late nights spent making our own voter guides, writing my own speeches, and crafting our own signs. We didn't have PAC money, but I knew we had something stronger: a shared sense of purpose, a burning conviction that fueled every late night, every phone call, every conversation. It was my purpose, and it became theirs.

One of my most significant contributions was my ability to leverage my grassroots organizing experience to engage diverse segments of the population. Understanding the nuanced needs and concerns of various communities within my constituency – I knew this intimately – enabled me to build broad-based support for my campaign. I demonstrated that community-based organizing principles could effectively translate into broader success for the community. My background provided a unique lens through which my community and I discussed and viewed policy challenges, enabling me to advocate for solutions that directly addressed the needs of those most affected. I saw firsthand how these policies impacted people's lives, and that fueled my passion to fight for change.

I also understood the importance of coalition-building across traditional political divides. Recognizing that environmental justice wasn't a partisan issue, my team and I collaborated with individuals from across the political spectrum to advance our campaign goals. I learned to find common ground, focusing on shared objectives and working towards mutually beneficial solutions, and saw firsthand that progress could be achieved through collaborative efforts. This cross-partisan approach proved instrumental in gaining support for my proposals.

The challenges I faced on the campaign trail were many and varied. I encountered opposition from powerful corporate interests, bureaucratic inertia, and the constant, swirling currents of political maneuvering. It was exhausting, frankly. Yet, I persevered, driven by my deep commitment to environmental justice and a fierce determination to navigate the complexities of the political system. I learned firsthand that the campaign trail demanded resilience, more determination than I ever thought I possessed, and an unwavering commitment to my principles – a commitment that was tested daily, sometimes hourly.

My commitment to transparency and accountability was paramount. I engaged in open dialogues with voters, regularly providing updates on my initiatives and seeking their input on decisions. This participatory approach built trust and fostered a sense of shared ownership on the campaign trail. It demonstrated to me that being an effective candidate required not only strong leadership but also genuine, collaborative engagement with the community.

This work is a powerful example of how I saw community organizing translate into real political action. In my experience, grassroots activism and formal politics aren't mutually exclusive, but complementary forces working together for significant change. This journey, a testament to the power of perseverance, coalition-building, and effective communication – all crucial in achieving meaningful change while keeping community empowerment at the heart of it all. I believe the legacy crafted and molded with love for the people will undoubtedly inspire future generations of activists and politicians.

Building effective political alliances wasn't simply a matter of networking; it demanded a deep understanding of the political landscape and the motivations of various players, something I learned firsthand. My initial attempts at collaboration were often met with skepticism. I could feel it – many established politicians viewed my grassroots background with suspicion, questioning my experience and political acumen. Others were wary of my unwavering commitment to environmental justice, fearing it might jeopardize their political agendas.

I knew I had to overcome this. Overcoming this initial resistance required a strategic approach. I began by identifying potential allies who shared my commitment to specific policy goals, regardless of their broader political affiliations. I focused on building relationships with legislators from both sides of the aisle, emphasizing common ground and shared objectives. This involved countless meetings, informal conversations, and behind-the-scenes negotiations – I spent hours in those back rooms. I actively sought out opportunities to collaborate on legislation that addressed overlapping concerns, demonstrating my willingness to compromise and build consensus. It wasn't easy; I had to learn to pick my battles and find the right points of leverage.

One particularly successful alliance emerged from an unexpected partnership with a conservative legislator known for his pro-business stance. While seemingly an unlikely ally, I saw an opportunity to open a dialogue. This legislator represented a rural district heavily reliant on tourism and agriculture, both of which were severely impacted by climate change. I worked with him, listening carefully to his concerns, to draft legislation that incentivized sustainable agricultural practices and promoted environmentally responsible tourism. This collaboration not only garnered bipartisan support for the city proposal but also demonstrated the broader appeal of environmentally conscious policies when framed in terms of economic benefits. It was a victory I felt deeply, a testament to the power of finding common ground with legislators at the local, state, and county levels.

This success proved the power of framing—I knew it! I learned to tailor my arguments, emphasizing the economic, social, and public health benefits of environmental protection to resonate with diverse audiences. I presented environmental justice not as a niche concern, but as a critical issue impacting everyone's well-being; I saw it as a matter of fundamental fairness and public health. I actively engaged with business leaders, showing them firsthand how environmentally sustainable practices could enhance their bottom line and increase their competitive advantage.

This approach helped me neutralize some of the opposition from corporate interests, building bridges where I'd previously seen only impassable divides. Building alliances also extended beyond the legislative sphere. I formed strong partnerships with environmental advocacy organizations, labor unions, and community groups—it felt like building a coalition of the willing. These partnerships provided crucial support during legislative battles, allowing for a coordinated and amplified advocacy campaign. I remember the thrill of those joint press conferences, the coordinated lobbying efforts, and the grassroots mobilization campaigns; they dramatically increased the visibility and impact of our legislative initiatives.

This collaborative approach transformed isolated efforts into a powerful collective force—something far greater than I could have achieved alone. The partnership with labor unions proved particularly significant. I knew many union members worked in industries directly affected by environmental regulations, and I understood their initial fears of job losses and economic hardship. Working closely with union leaders, I helped craft legislation that protected workers' rights while promoting environmental sustainability. This approach demonstrated my commitment to balancing environmental protection with social justice concerns, neutralizing potential opposition, and transforming potential adversaries into strong allies. I felt a tremendous sense of accomplishment seeing that happen.

Beyond formal alliances, I understood the importance of fostering informal networks of support. I cultivated relationships with legislative staff members, building trust and rapport with individuals who played crucial roles in the legislative process. These relationships proved invaluable in navigating the complexities of the legislative system, obtaining critical information, and securing support for the initiatives crafted by the needs and concerns of my community. My ability to build personal connections proved as effective, if not more so, than formal alliances. Maintaining these alliances required continuous effort and compromise. I understood that political partnerships were not static arrangements but rather dynamic relationships requiring ongoing negotiation and adjustment.

I remained committed to my core principles, but I also demonstrated flexibility and a willingness to seek common ground, even on issues where I initially held strong opposing views. This flexibility wasn't a betrayal of my values but a pragmatic approach to achieving meaningful progress. The process wasn't always easy. Internal conflicts within alliances were inevitable, stemming from differing priorities and strategies. I skillfully navigated these conflicts, facilitating dialogue and finding compromises that maintained the integrity of the alliance while addressing the concerns of its members. This involved active listening, empathy, and a willingness to compromise without sacrificing my core beliefs.

Successfully navigating the complexities of political and community alliances, bringing community into the halls of legislators, demanded strong communication skills, something I knew needed mastery. I was adept at articulating my vision, clearly communicating my goals and strategies, and I made a point of actively listening to the perspectives of my allies. I fostered open communication channels, ensuring that I heard everyone and that all members of the alliance felt heard and valued. This transparency, I found, built trust and facilitated productive collaborations. Moreover, my success in building alliances rested on my commitment to transparency and accountability. I kept my partners informed of my progress, actively sought their input on key decisions, and I always made sure to share credit for our successes. This approach fostered a sense of shared ownership and strengthened the bonds within the alliance. It also enhanced my credibility and built trust – crucial components for sustained collaboration, and something I prioritized from the start.

The formation and maintenance of political alliances became a cornerstone of my success. I learned that effective political action often required navigating intricate relationships, building bridges across ideological divides, and leveraging the power of collective action.

My ability to forge strong and enduring alliances transformed me from a grassroots activist into a formidable political force capable of achieving meaningful change. This ability to build consensus, find common ground, and leverage the power of diverse partnerships stands as a powerful testament to my political acumen and my unwavering dedication to environmental justice. My story underscores the crucial role of coalition-building in transforming political vision into tangible progress – a lesson I learned on the campaign trail.

My campaign, though it fell short of electoral victory, ignited a profound and unexpected transformation within our California community. The loss, while deeply felt, became a crucible forging a new understanding of power and influence. I came to realize that my true power wasn't confined to the gilded cage of a congressional seat; it resided in the very heart of the people, in the unwavering commitment to the principles I championed, and in the messy, beautiful process of collective action itself. This epiphany spurred a profound shift in my purpose, a re-calibration of my compass towards a higher calling. I found myself becoming, not a politician seeking office, but a conduit, a bridge spanning the chasm between the unheard voices of our community and the often-distant, sometimes deaf ears of political power brokers.

This bridge-building found its most potent expression during the agonizingly crucial redistricting process in my hometown of Ontario. Across the nation, the redrawing of electoral maps was unfolding, but in Ontario, I saw it not as a mere procedural exercise, but as a battle for the very soul of our democracy, a fight for the visibility, equity, and fundamental sense of belonging that had been denied for far too long. The maps, crafted in the shadows, in backrooms shielded from public scrutiny, were designed to protect the entrenched power of incumbents, to further marginalize already vulnerable communities. But my nonprofit and I refused to allow this travesty to unfold without resistance. We embarked on a journey fueled by courage, resilience, and a deep-seated conviction in the power of the people. We organized, not merely mobilized, but truly *activated* our neighborhoods, awakening a slumbering giant, a collective will that refused to be silenced or ignored. The experience was a profound lesson in the power of grassroots activism and a testament to the enduring human spirit in the face of formidable odds. The fight itself, the very act of defiance, became a victory in its own right, etching a deeper understanding of justice and representation into the fabric of our community.

The air in the council chambers crackled. Not with electricity, but with the hushed anticipation of a hundred breaths held. On the table, our map lay spread – a vibrant tapestry woven from countless stories, each colored pin a life, a shared laugh, a whispered worry. Youth, their faces alight with newfound power, presented the data, their voices clear and strong in Spanish, Mandarin, Punjabi – the languages of our community.

Grandmothers, their hands gnarled but firm, clutched translated pamphlets, their testimony a low, steady hum of lived experience. We'd spent months in this very room, weeks in community centers, hours at kitchen tables, listening, translating, painstakingly plotting the lives that made up our city.

The council members shifted, papers rustling, the quiet murmur of their consultations a counterpoint to the heartbeats thrumming in the room. Then, the gavel fell. A unanimous "aye." A wave of relief, so potent it was almost physical, washed over us. Not just a victory, but a seismic shift. We hadn't just influenced the process; we'd rewritten the rules. The scent of victory –sharp, sweet, and indelible – lingered long after the meeting adjourned.

Later, the sterile fluorescence of the Mountain View School Board meeting felt jarringly different. But the feeling, the work, was the same. I remember the sharp intake of breath from a board member when a young mother, her voice trembling slightly with emotion, described how the proposed lines would split her child's community. "This isn't about numbers," she said, her voice rising, "it's about our children's futures." The quiet power in her words – a stark contrast to the cold data on the charts – shifted the atmosphere. We'd brought the fight, the compassion, the same unwavering belief that every child deserved a school reflecting their life, their community, their identity.

Redistricting? To them, a technicality. To us, a sacred act. Each line drawn, a decision about who got a voice, who got power, who got heard. In city halls, in school board rooms, we'd stared those lines in the face, fought to redraw them, fought for justice – one meticulously placed pin, one impassioned voice, one hard-won victory at a time. The weight of those lines, the lives they shaped, the futures they determined – the responsibility had been heavy. But the victory? That was heavier still.

This journey etched deeply into my soul the profound truth that true power transcends the confines of elected office. It resides in the unwavering act of organizing, in the courageous articulation of truth, and in the painstaking construction of alliances that endure beyond fleeting headlines. Our campaign wasn't merely a deployment of strategies and data; it was an outpouring of presence, a tapestry woven from shared stories and the unwavering strength of families. We humanized the political process, forcing the system to confront the very people it was designed to serve.

Reflecting on this chapter, I don't mourn a lost campaign; I celebrate a movement ignited. The flames of that movement continue to burn brightly today. Young organizers throughout the Inland Empire are now crafting policy, leading their own redistricting battles, and forging coalitions that are reshaping California from within. The path of policy change is undeniably slow, a tortuous and often messy process. Yet, when grounded in the bedrock of community, it becomes an unstoppable force, a river carving its way through stone. I may not have personally penned the laws, but I played a vital role in redrawing the political map, thereby reshaping our collective future.

The Community Coalition's words resonate with profound meaning: "Melissa May didn't need a seat in Congress to move the system. She just needed a community that believed." And believe they did. Together, we achieved the seemingly impossible, moving mountains and constructing new ones in their stead. The electoral outcome didn't define the impact of our campaign; instead, it kindled a powerful fire within me, igniting a movement for environmental justice across California. I discovered that my influence extended far beyond the prospect of a congressional seat. By immersing myself in the heart of the community, I became a bridge, connecting the voices of those suffering from environmental injustice with the policymakers empowered to enact change. This became my purpose, my passion, my driving force.

I consulted, I collaborated, sharing my knowledge and experience with environmental justice organizations and grassroots coalitions. We toiled tirelessly, shaping legislation, crafting compelling testimonies, and forging unbreakable alliances. Through the unification of diverse groups, we created a potent force that swept across the Inland Empire and beyond, influencing policies and dramatically improving the lives of those bearing the brunt of environmental injustices. Legislative change is undeniably a slow, arduous climb, but when fueled by the unwavering spirit of the community, it becomes an irresistible force. I may not have written the laws, but I profoundly shaped their creation. I may not have won the election, but I reshaped the very landscape of the political arena.

Today, I witness the fruits of our collective labor. Young organizers across California are not merely bearing witness; they are leading campaigns, providing crucial consultation, and crafting policy from the inside. They embody the future, and I am deeply honored to have played even a small part in their journey. As I reflect on this deeply personal and profoundly rewarding experience, I am humbled anew by the Community Coalition's simple yet powerful statement: "Melissa May didn't need a seat in Congress to move the system. She just needed a community that believed." My community did believe, and together, we moved mountains.

The ascent from the echoing frustration of a school auditorium, filled with parents' anxieties, to the heady, terrifying heights of reshaping political power across an entire city felt less like a climb and more like navigating a labyrinth forged from layers of unseen obstacles. Bureaucracy, cloaked in secrecy and whispered deals, formed the chilling bedrock; deep-rooted inequities, the treacherous, shifting sands. The exhaustion was a physical weight, the discouragement a constant, gnawing companion. My success wasn't a matter of fortune; it was the hard-won fruit of witnessing, firsthand, the unwavering, often unseen, commitment it takes to crack the shell of a civic system designed, it seemed, to mute the voices it purported to represent. That was the profound, unsettling revelation: grassroots mobilization and formal politics aren't parallel tracks, diverging into separate destinies; they are inextricably linked, two currents of the same urgent river, both necessary to force the dam of inertia to break.

Redistricting became my crucible, my proving ground, and my unexpected blueprint for change. Stepping into that process, first for the City of Ontario, then for the Mountain View School Board, I understood I wasn't merely sketching lines on a map; I was sketching the very architecture of power itself, a power that shapes lives in ways most people never truly grasp. Those lines, seemingly innocuous, dictate everything: the flow of school funding, the distribution of city resources, the strength of environmental protections, the very composition of our representative bodies. Gerrymandered maps, I learned, are instruments of silencing, capable of stifling entire communities for a decade or more. But when crafted with unwavering integrity and a deep respect for the communities they serve, redistricting emerges as one of the most potent tools for achieving justice within a democracy, a means of ensuring every voice, however faint, can be heard, and every concern, however seemingly small, can finally find a place at the table. That's why I poured my heart and soul into mobilizing my non-profit, igniting the passion of our volunteers, and embarking on a mission to empower local residents with the knowledge to navigate the redistricting process—a process often deliberately obfuscated to suppress participation. We peeled back the layers of deception, demystifying the complexities. We held community forums, tirelessly translated vital documents, collaborated with legal experts, and patiently guided our community to decipher population data, identify the insidious manipulations of gerrymandering, and, ultimately, draft their own maps. This was far more than redrawing lines on a page; it was about reclaiming the fundamental power that had been systematically denied to those who had been so long ignored, their voices silenced.

The formal political arena proved a grueling battleground. City council meetings bled into the night, stretching our resolve to its limits. Procedural maneuvers were weaponized as tools of delay, designed to exhaust and ultimately defeat us. Yet, we possessed a strategy forged in the fires of shared purpose. We painstakingly built a map *with* the people, *for* the people—a map grounded in the principles of fairness, cultural preservation, and authentic representation. We didn't just submit this map; we submitted it alongside a tapestry of stories. Stories of children walking miles to school, their futures hanging in the balance. Stories of elders, marginalized and ignored at the polls for decades, their wisdom and experience dismissed. Stories of mothers yearning for a voice, desperate to be heard within the district they called home. We made it abundantly clear: our map was not merely a proposal; it was a clarion call for justice, a demand that could no longer be ignored.

And, against all odds, the city council listened. Despite the intense pressure from entrenched incumbents, clinging desperately to the status quo, they voted to approve the community-crafted map. This was more than a victory; it was a watershed moment, a historic triumph. But this success didn't emerge in a vacuum. It was the product of a powerful synergy, a potent fusion of grassroots mobilization and shrewd political strategy. We mastered the rules of engagement, not to manipulate the system, but to harness its power, aligning it with the unwavering will of our people. It was a testament to the enduring power of collective action, a beacon of hope demonstrating what can be achieved when the marginalized find their voice and the silenced refuse to be ignored.

My role evolved. I wasn't merely an advocate; I became a mentor, a strategist, a weaver of alliances, a bridge between the disenfranchised and the halls of power. I didn't just teach others to challenge power structures; I empowered them to reshape them. I guided local coalitions, hand-holding them through the intricacies of public records requests, the art of strategic pressure, the crucial translation of raw data into compelling, actionable demands. I worked shoulder-to-shoulder with families, elders, young people—first-time advocates blossoming before my eyes. They weren't merely empowered; they were ignited, their spirits blazing with a newfound agency.

Witnessing the transformative power of civic education interwoven with shrewd political strategy was a revelation. The anger, the righteous fury, was vital, but it was the organization, the meticulous planning, that converted that energy into tangible results.

Knowing the truth wasn't enough; we had to present it with such compelling force that institutions were compelled to respond, to change course. This wasn't simply a local victory in Ontario or Mountain View; it became a blueprint, a beacon of hope for cities grappling with their own redistricting battles—a testament to the profound possibility, the undeniable necessity, of community-led governance.

This wasn't simply a redrawing of political lines; it was a profound reclaiming of our collective identity, a painstaking restoration of a history deliberately obscured, and a courageous forging of a future where justice and equity were not mere aspirations but lived realities. The ripple effect of our work, a legacy echoing across generations, filled me with a deep and abiding sense of purpose. To witness young organizers, their hands now steady on the map, their voices ringing with newfound power in state hearings, leading advocacy groups and building inclusive spaces where everyone truly belongs – this is the tangible fruit of the seeds we sowed together, a testament to the power of shared vision. I brought more than data to the table; I brought the stories, the faces, the families – the very heart of the struggle – and the strategic framework to amplify their voices, transforming raw pain into potent political action.

Redistricting, in its complexity and intensity, imparted a lesson no campaign or election ever could: true, lasting change doesn't always arrive with the fanfare of victory, a title, or a seat in office. Sometimes, it arrives quietly, powerfully, with a carefully drawn map, a shared vision, and a community brave enough to demand a better world. This experience revealed to me that power doesn't reside with those who cling to it jealously, but with those who dare to reimagine it, to reclaim it, line by painstaking line, block by determined block, heart by fiercely beating heart—a process that demands unwavering courage and relentless dedication.

This commitment extended far beyond redistricting. I actively mentored younger activists, sharing knowledge and skills, fostering the next generation of environmental advocates.

This underscores a crucial truth: lasting social change isn't solely dependent on individual efforts; it necessitates the nurturing of future generations, the passing of the torch to those who will carry the fight forward. Sustainable progress relies on the collective efforts of numerous individuals across multiple generations. Our legacy isn't solely in the legislative achievements we attained, but in the individuals we inspired, empowering them to lead us toward an even brighter future.

True political engagement transcends the simple act of voting or donating to campaigns. It's about actively shaping the political discourse, mobilizing public support, and forging powerful collaborations to achieve shared goals. It demands a deep understanding of the political landscape, the intricacies of policy-making, and the art of building consensus even across deeply divided lines. It's about employing diverse communication strategies to inform and persuade, building bridges across ideological divides, and forging compromises that address the concerns of all stakeholders. It is the vital bridge connecting the impassioned calls for change from the grassroots to the concrete actions necessary to transform those calls into a tangible reality. This synergistic approach, honed and perfected by my team, serves as a potent model for future activists seeking meaningful social and environmental transformation.

My memoir aims to serve as a blueprint for future activists, demonstrating the transformative potential that arises when grassroots mobilization meets strategic political action. This integrated approach isn't merely a tactic; it's a fundamental necessity for achieving lasting positive change in any area of social or environmental concern. It's a testament to the power of people uniting their voices, their energy, their intellect, and their unwavering determination to effect profound and lasting change in the world through the implementation of a comprehensive and strategically sound plan of action.

Chapter 6:

A Legacy of Change

L ooking back, the path hasn't been a straight line. It's been a winding road—full of unexpected turns, steep inclines, and valleys that tested my resolve more than once. There were moments of profound discouragement, when the weight of injustice felt like it would crush any hope of real reform. The battles against entrenched power structures, the deliberate misinformation campaigns, the seemingly endless negotiations to be heard without compromising our principles—these moments were some of the greatest tests of endurance in my life.

And yet, amidst the struggles, there were moments of exhilarating triumph. I witnessed firsthand the power of organized, collective action. I saw maps—once designed to silence communities—redrawn by the very people they tried to exclude. I saw neighborhoods, long overlooked, finally come together with pride and purpose. I saw young activists step up and speak truth to power with clarity and courage. Those were the moments when the seeds of change blossomed into something real, something transformational.

One of the most significant lessons I learned is that no victory in redistricting or environmental justice comes alone. Early in my journey, I believed that activism meant fighting solo—one voice shouting into the void. I was wrong. Our success in securing community-made maps in both the City of Ontario and the Mountain View School Board, and our continued push for equitable environmental justice policies, stemmed from coalition-building: the collective strength of neighbors, teachers, professors, students, parents, scientists, and spiritual leaders working shoulder to shoulder. Real change wasn't born from one person's fire—it came from fanning thousands of flames until the whole system began to glow with the possibility of something better.

These coalitions didn't form by accident. They were rooted in deep listening—understanding each group's specific concerns, histories, and visions for justice. In the redistricting process, that meant translating census data and legal jargon into meaningful community conversations. It meant understanding how gerrymandered lines had fractured neighborhoods and divided voices for decades—and then imagining, together, what fair representation could look like. For environmental justice, it meant recognizing how pollution, zoning decisions, and lack of access to green space disproportionately harmed Black, Indigenous, and working-class communities—and then organizing for policies that didn't just fix a problem, but healed historical wounds.

I learned that technical skill and data were necessary, but not sufficient. What truly shifted the tide was the power of storytelling. Not just charts and maps, but people—their breath, their grief, their dreams. I made sure every public hearing included testimony from mothers whose children had suffered asthma due to warehouse pollution, from students who had never seen a single tree planted near their schools, from elders who remembered a time when their community had a say in what was built around them. These stories humanized the issues and created emotional resonance that cut through political posturing. They made injustice undeniable—and action unavoidable.

The media played a critical role in amplifying our message. We built social media campaigns with vibrant visuals, shared real-time updates from public meetings, and turned legal wins into viral victories. From traditional newspapers to digital platforms, we ensured our voices couldn't be ignored. Infographics made census blocks feel personal. Videos of community testimony moved hearts. And most importantly, we created two-way conversations—soliciting feedback, answering questions, and adapting our strategies based on what our people needed most.

I also came to understand that change requires sustained engagement. Winning a vote was never the finish line—it was the foundation. We created long-term action plans that evolved with the political landscape. Whether it was monitoring the implementation of a new voting map or ensuring environmental justice funds reached the communities most impacted, we stayed vigilant. We learned to expect setbacks, to read the room, to pivot with purpose—but never to retreat.

That's why mentorship became a core part of my work. I wasn't just fighting to pass policy or approve maps—I was planting seeds for the next generation of change-makers. I mentored student leaders, trained emerging organizers and political candidates, and created tools they could adapt for their own communities. I believe that real legacy is not measured by what you build alone, but by who you inspire to build alongside you. My deepest hope is that every person I've walked with on this journey will one day lead their own movements, using what we created as their foundation.

The challenges are still vast. The fight for environmental justice, fair representation, and equitable policymaking is far from over. But as I reflect on the road behind me, I do so with profound hope. Because I've seen what's possible when communities are empowered, when stories are honored, and when activism is grounded in both heart and strategy. More than any map, ordinance, or policy, it's the transformation of people—from witnesses to warriors—that defines the true impact of this journey.

This is what it means to move from protest to power. To turn redistricting into resistance. To turn justice from a dream into a design. And most of all, to know that the journey continues—not because we must, but because we can. Together.

The passage of the community-led redistricting plans and environmental justice reforms marked significant victories, but their long-term impact extends far beyond the initial moment of achievement. The vote, the legislation, the map adoption—these were merely entry points. The true measure of success lies in sustained implementation, community empowerment, and vigilant accountability.

Redistricting and environmental justice are not one-time events; they are processes that demand ongoing participation, consistent monitoring, and strategic adaptation. For redistricting, this means ensuring that newly drawn maps are honored in practice—that fair representation leads to responsive governance. For environmental justice, it means continued enforcement of regulations, the dismantling of environmental racism in land-use decisions, and the reallocation of public investments to communities long ignored. The energy of the initial victory must be transformed into a long-term commitment, ensuring the promises we fought for are not symbolic, but deeply transformative.

A central component of this transformation is the creation of effective monitoring and evaluation mechanisms. Passing a policy or approving a district map is only the beginning; what comes next determines whether real change will be felt on the ground. We must build robust systems for tracking impact—ensuring public access to data, community feedback loops, and transparent reporting. In redistricting, that means auditing voter access, reviewing turnout data across neighborhoods, and assessing whether elected officials now better reflect the diversity and needs of their constituents. In environmental justice, it means tracking warehouse permits, air quality, zoning patterns, and enforcement of pollution regulations, particularly in frontline communities. The data must be dynamic, accessible to communities (by training community leaders in the analysis and implementation of actionable steps the community can implement immediately) and used to inform continual improvement, not sit dormant on bureaucratic shelves.

But technical systems alone aren't enough. The success of these long-term initiatives is intimately tied to the capacity of local communities to lead and sustain them. That's why we invest in civic education, participatory planning, and leadership training. We don't just want fair maps or cleaner neighborhoods—we want communities to understand their rights, exercise their power, and steward these wins for future generations. In Ontario and throughout California's Inland Empire, our efforts trained everyday residents—parents, students, elders—to read maps, testify at hearings, and draft their own proposals. This democratization of knowledge became our strongest defense against backroom deals and top-down policies.

Beyond the structural wins, the societal ripple effects must be acknowledged. Equitable redistricting and environmental justice policy directly impact public health, voter trust, and long-term social stability. Cleaner neighborhoods reduce asthma and cancer rates. Fair maps empower people to elect leaders who reflect their values. Together, these changes lead to lower healthcare costs, better school attendance, stronger community participation, and a greater sense of belonging. Though harder to measure, these ripple effects are no less real—and they reveal the profound return on investment that comes from putting power back into the hands of the people most affected.

We've also learned that long-term transformation requires systemic reinvestment—in infrastructure, in people, and in the political imagination. It's not enough to redraw a map or pass a new ordinance; we must back it with public funds, sustainable policy enforcement, and continued community input. That means establishing resident-led planning boards, redirecting budgets toward frontline neighborhoods, and embedding environmental justice principles into every department—from transportation to housing to public health.

Public engagement remains central to all of this. We must continue to educate, mobilize, and co-create with the very communities we serve. We've hosted voter empowerment trainings, conducted map literacy workshops, and launched storytelling campaigns to show the human face behind zoning decisions and voter lines, how neighbors and schools are directly impacted when families, friends, and neighbors are broken apart from one another during the redistricting process. We've used social media, art, and short-form videos to make environmental racism visible and actionable. The fight is not just legal—it is cultural. It requires changing narratives, building trust, and anchoring people in the belief that their voice matters.

And we are not naïve. We know progress can be undone. That's why we push for legal safeguards—policies with teeth, transparency provisions, and community oversight councils. We know political winds shift. Redistricting reforms can be challenged, environmental protections rolled back. So we create institutions and coalitions resilient enough to hold the line and push forward even in hard times. It's not about hoping for the best—it's about preparing, defending, and evolving our strategies, but resources like funding, training, and access to media are essential to ensuring equitable outcomes.

Central to that evolution is the next generation. We are not simply building policy—we are building people. We mentor high school students on how to run public comment campaigns. We train college interns to analyze zoning ordinances. We host community retreats where young leaders design the neighborhoods they want to inherit. This isn't extracurricular—it's essential. The long arc of justice needs continuity, and that only happens when we pass the torch with intention.

Looking ahead, the challenges remain daunting. Climate change, voter suppression, gentrification, corporate lobbying—all pose real and growing threats. But we are not where we started. The redistricting victories we fought for—rooted in equity, language access, and demographic truth—now serve as models for other cities. The environmental justice work we advanced continues to shape statewide funding priorities and public health frameworks.

Our legacy will not be measured by the number of maps we drew or meetings we attended. It will be measured by the empowerment of everyday people, the transformation of power structures, and the cultural shift toward justice, equity, and sustainability. We have planted seeds in city councils, classrooms, and courtrooms. And as those seeds take root and grow, we continue onward—tending the soil, defending the progress, and making space for others to rise.

The journey is far from over. But the foundation is strong. The will of the people is resilient. And our collective vision for a just and sustainable future remains crystal clear. Let those who come after us say: they didn't just change policy—they changed the culture of the powerless to empowered.

The success of our redistricting victories and environmental justice campaigns hinges not only on policy wins, but on the cultivation of a vibrant, informed, and empowered citizenry—especially among young people. Legislation opens the door, but it's culture that keeps it open. Sustainable change requires more than government votes; it requires generational commitment. To secure a just and equitable future, we must deliberately invest in the leadership of tomorrow—those who will inherit our maps, our air, our waters, our neighborhoods, and our movements.

This work begins with education, yes—but it cannot stop at curriculum. While integrating environmental justice and civic education into classrooms is essential, it is only one thread in a much larger tapestry. We must create pathways to real-world engagement, where students transform learning into lived action. This means inviting youth into the heart of civic life—not as passive observers, but as active participants and community stewards.

One of the most powerful strategies we employed was supporting youth-led initiatives. These spaces allowed young people to take ownership of local issues—from analyzing draft redistricting maps to organizing community forums on warehouse pollution. Through these efforts, they didn't just study policy— they shaped it. Youth-led organizing became a fertile training ground for advocacy, teaching critical skills like consensus-building, finding common ground with those who might be in opposition, public speaking, data analysis, and ethical leadership.

These young advocates emerged not just as students, but as strategists, as collaborators, and as defenders of democracy and the earth. Mentorship became another cornerstone of our work. We intentionally built intergenerational alliances, pairing young leaders with policy experts, legal advocates, environmental scientists, and organizers who could guide them. Mentorship wasn't hierarchical—it was relational. Our goal was to pass on not just knowledge, but courage, humility, and vision. Whether walking them through public comment processes or reviewing map proposals side by side, we built a culture of support that honored both experience and fresh perspective. This created a sense of belonging and continuity, where wisdom flowed in both directions.

We also created robust internship and volunteer programs within our nonprofit coalition, placing young people in decision-making spaces—from city planning committees to neighborhood canvassing operations. They gained hands-on experience in redistricting analysis, public outreach, environmental monitoring, and policy advocacy. They learned how to run meetings, mobilize communities, and write testimony. In doing so, they realized that power is not a distant concept—it's something they could touch, hold, and wield with integrity at a young age. By building awareness, confidence, wisdom, and discernment within our youth, we built resilience, resolve, and reliability in the next pillar of our community.

Equally important was creating space—literal and symbolic—for young people to express their truths and shape the narrative. Whether through youth advisory boards, listening sessions, or public storytelling events, we invited youth into conversations where decisions were made. When I coordinated the Rising Voices Conference in 2023 at the Ontario Convention Center, we did exactly this—centering youth as thought leaders, not just attendees, who gave presentations of the data they collected around the issues they were organizing and developing policy for. City Council, business leaders, and diverse members of the community attended these youth-led presentations at the Rising Voices Conference. These platforms allowed their insights to be heard, their concerns legitimized, and their creative visions welcomed as part of the broader policy dialogue.

College and University institutions played a vital role in this movement. We worked closely with schools and colleges to expand environmental justice and civic education—not as isolated electives, but as cross-disciplinary lenses. We showed how redistricting intersects with history, how zoning impacts health, how climate justice connects to economics and ethics. Through project-based learning, college students conducted research, designed campaigns, and proposed community solutions. Education was no longer theoretical—it became urgent, embodied, and deeply personal.

The role of the media was undeniable. We leaned into storytelling—videos, podcasts, short films—to elevate the voices of young advocates. We helped them produce content that was bold, bilingual, and accessible. Their work reached thousands and inspired countless others to believe that change was not only possible—it was already happening, and they were part of it. The power of visibility ignited a feedback loop: the more they were seen, the more they spoke; the more they spoke, the more others joined in.

But we also knew this work could not be colorblind or class-neutral. We intentionally addressed the barriers that marginalized communities face in accessing civic power and environmental safety. We worked to break down those barriers—by translating materials, offering stipends, holding events in trusted community spaces, and naming the legacies of environmental racism and voter suppression for what they are. Justice was not an add-on—it was our starting point.

The truth is, the young people who joined our movement are not just environmentalists or voting rights advocates—they are visionaries. They are shaping the next evolution of social justice: one rooted in solidarity, intersectionality, and systemic transformation. These are the leaders who will demand clean water and fair housing. Who will fight for accessible healthcare and healthy neighborhoods. Who will rebuild cities with equity at the center, not as a slogan, but as a lived principle.

This is why inspiring future leaders is not a luxury—it is a strategic imperative. It is how we secure the gains we've made and ensure they are not erased by the next wave of political turnover. It is how we turn moments into movements, and policies into culture. The work of redistricting and environmental justice does not end with new maps or emissions caps. It continues in classrooms, on sidewalks, in courtrooms, and across ballot boxes— where a new generation rises not only to inherit the work, but to deepen and expand it.

To them, we leave more than policies—we leave a blueprint for transformation. We offer mentorship, tools, space, and most of all—our belief in their brilliance. The journey forward belongs to them. But the story they will write is being shaped now, with each opportunity we provide, each barrier we remove, and each spark of possibility we ignite in their hearts.

The fight for environmental justice and equitable representation is not a sprint—it is a marathon. It demands steadfast devotion, strategic evolution, and an ever-renewing well of courage. While redistricting victories and environmental policy gains mark pivotal moments in the journey, they are not the destination. They are sacred milestones—stepping stones in a longer arc toward justice, equity, and sustainability. The true legacy of these achievements will be measured not only by their passage, but by the sustained momentum and widened circle of community voices they empower.

A core pillar of this long-term vision is persistent community accountability and impact evaluation. No policy, no matter how well-crafted, can fulfill its promise unless it is grounded in real-life feedback, measurable outcomes, and the lived experience of those most impacted. This means ensuring that redistricting maps are not just legally compliant, but community-centered—and that environmental regulations are followed by rigorous monitoring, transparent data-sharing, adequate funding, and course correction when outcomes fall short.

That's why we advocated for the formation of independent community oversight committees—composed not just of experts, but of the very residents whose lives are shaped by these policies. These bodies serve as a moral compass, ensuring public input is not a one-time checkbox but an ongoing dialogue. When data reveals that certain neighborhoods still suffer disproportionately from pollution or political exclusion, these community watchdogs can demand the recalibration of public policy, ensuring justice remains alive—not only in the text of the law but in its implementation.

We must also remain vigilant. The very forces that pollute our skies, suppress our votes, and extract resources from our communities are tenacious—and well-funded. Their tactics evolve, but so must ours. Sustaining our wins requires perpetual public engagement: showing up at hearings, submitting public comment, organizing voter education campaigns, and pushing back against attempts to undermine hard-won protections.

Our coalitions must remain nimble and deeply rooted, prepared to defend our progress with facts, voices, and people power. But this work cannot exist in silos. To create lasting transformation, we must embrace a multidimensional approach—one that simultaneously empowers communities, educates the public, and nurtures economic justice.

Empowerment starts with resources: legal support, translation services, access to environmental data, and training in advocacy tools. When we place power directly in the hands of residents, they become not just beneficiaries of reform, but architects of it. That's how we create durable solutions that reflect the richness, wisdom, and complexity of each unique community.

Education remains a cornerstone. True environmental and democratic literacy isn't passive—it's participatory. We must cultivate it not only in classrooms but on porches, at local libraries, in barbershops, and in community centers. Our goal is not merely to inform, but to ignite. We need campaigns that build curiosity, deepen analysis, and inspire action.

From school board meetings to city council chambers, we are raising a generation of residents who know their power—and how to use it.

Crucially, environmental justice must be woven into economic frameworks, not pitted against them. We need to reject models that treat clean air, safe housing, or accessible water as burdens or afterthoughts. Instead, we must champion policies that link equity with innovation: green job creation, workforce transition programs, sustainable infrastructure, and public investments that uplift historically neglected communities. Progress means nothing if it leaves the most vulnerable behind. True environmental and redistricting justice must redistribute opportunity, not just redraw boundaries.

To move forward, we must reckon with the past. For decades—indeed, centuries—marginalized communities have been deliberately zoned into harm: next to freeways, warehouses, power plants, and toxic dumping grounds. They've been written out of maps, silenced in hearings, and excluded from the rooms where decisions were made.

Justice demands that we confront these truths head-on. That we listen, repair, and redistribute—not out of guilt, but out of moral clarity and sacred responsibility.

Technology has a role to play—but only when it serves community need, not control. Tools like mapping software, air monitors, and data visualization platforms can democratize information—but only when they are made accessible, transparent, and used to support—not surveil—those on the frontlines. Tech must be our tool, not our replacement. No single city or state can do this alone. The scope of environmental injustice and political disempowerment is global. That's why we must remain active in international conversations and solidarity movements, exchanging models, lifting up shared struggles, and building transnational strategies. The solutions we need are interconnected—just like the harms we resist.

Intergenerational collaboration is key. We are not the first to fight this fight—and we will not be the last. Elders carry the scars and stories of past resistance. Youth carry fresh vision and boundless energy. Together, they form a sacred continuum. When we foster intentional spaces for their voices to meet, mentor, and co-create, we ensure that this movement does not fade—it evolves. What we pass on is not just knowledge, but the flame of purpose itself.

Collaboration is our most powerful tool. No one institution, sector, or individual can solve these challenges alone. We must deepen partnerships across nonprofits, agencies, tribal nations, academic institutions, and everyday neighbors. Our collective strength lies in our shared resolve, and in the diversity of our approaches, talents, and lived experiences.

And through it all, we must commit to continuous learning. No movement survives by standing still. Environmental conditions, political landscapes, and technological tools are always shifting. That's why we must be honest about what's working, unafraid to pivot, and always willing to listen. Reflection is not a luxury—it is a discipline of transformation.

This journey—at its core—is about love. Love for the land, for our neighbors, for our children's right to breathe freely and be counted fully. The legacy of this work is written not only in court victories or legislation, but in healed communities, empowered youth, and a planet that breathes easier because of our care.

The fight for environmental justice continues—not because we have failed, but because we have succeeded in igniting hope. It is our responsibility now to protect that flame and grow it. To ensure that the pathways we've cleared remain open and that the seeds we've planted are watered by future hands.

This is our collective story, our collective duty. And together, with unshakable love and sacred conviction, we will finish the race we began.

The journey towards environmental justice is far from over. The victories we've celebrated—the legislative wins, the community-led initiatives, the technological advancements—are not an endpoint but rather crucial milestones on a long and winding road. The legacy of this movement will be defined not just by the policies enacted but by the sustained commitment and active participation of individuals like yourselves. This isn't a passive endeavor; it demands active engagement, a willingness to step outside our comfort zones, and a dedication to making a tangible difference in the world.

So, what can you do? The answer, thankfully, is multifaceted. Your contribution, however small it may seem, can have a ripple effect, inspiring others and accelerating the pace of change.

First and foremost, educate yourself. Environmental justice is a complex issue, encompassing a vast array of interconnected challenges. Immerse yourself in the literature. Read reports from organizations like, the Union of Concerned Scientists, California Environmental Justice Alliance (CEJA), CAL EPA, and Earthjustice. Familiarize yourself with the scientific data, understand the historical context, and grasp the intricate web of social, economic, and political factors that contribute to environmental inequities. Knowledge is power, and an informed citizenry is the bedrock of any successful movement for social change. This includes understanding the specific environmental challenges impacting your own community—are there disproportionate levels of air or water pollution? Are there specific industries contributing to environmental degradation in your area? What are the historical patterns of environmental injustice that have shaped your community's current reality? Which politicians are accepting campaign donations from corporations and special interests - which do more harm than good for your community?

Next, engage in your community. Environmental justice is not a distant, abstract concept; it's woven into the fabric of our daily lives. Start by participating in local environmental initiatives. Volunteer with organizations working to clean up polluted waterways, plant trees, or advocate for stronger environmental regulations by attending your City, County, and State meetings. Meet with your congressional representatives to ask them about their goals and plans to pass legislation that encompasses Environmental Justice. Attend community meetings and town halls, voicing your concerns and offering your support and expertise. Connect with local environmental groups, learn about their work, and contribute your skills and talents. If you don't see an organization addressing the specific environmental injustices in your community, consider starting one. The power of collective action should not be underestimated.

Advocate for policy change. Contact your elected officials—at the local, state, and national levels—to express your support for strong environmental protections and environmental justice policies. Write letters, make phone calls, and attend public forums. Urge them to prioritize environmental justice in their decision-making. Support candidates who champion environmental protection and advocate for policies that address environmental inequities. Remember, your voice matters, and elected officials are more responsive when they hear from their constituents who turn out to vote. Your vote is your voice, and it carries immense power to enact change for the common good. Elected officials look at voter rolls and take the comments and testimonies of those who vote in every single election, every single time, seriously. These people are called high propensity voters. This is where most politicians and candidates spend most of their campaign money, targeting and conducting outreach to high propensity voters.

Support organizations fighting for environmental justice. Many organizations are dedicated to advancing environmental justice, conducting research, providing legal assistance, and organizing communities. Contribute financially to these groups; even a small donation can make a significant difference. Volunteer your time to help with their advocacy and outreach efforts. Spread the word about their work, encouraging others to support their mission.

Consider becoming a member of these organizations, strengthening their base of support and amplifying their collective voice by sharing their messaging and work on social media.

Challenge environmental racism and injustice. Environmental justice is inherently intertwined with social justice. Actively challenge the systemic racism, classism, and other forms of discrimination that contribute to environmental inequities. Speak out against polluting industries that disproportionately affect marginalized communities. Support initiatives aimed at promoting economic empowerment and community development in environmentally vulnerable areas. This active confrontation of injustice is crucial in moving beyond mere awareness to meaningful and sustainable change.

Support sustainable businesses and practices. Make conscious choices in your daily life that support environmental sustainability. Reduce your carbon footprint by using public transportation, cycling, or walking. Choose to buy locally sourced, organic food whenever possible, or create your own victory garden or community garden. Reduce your consumption of single-use plastics and buy reusable canteens. Support businesses that prioritize environmental sustainability and social responsibility. Individual actions, when multiplied by widespread adoption, ignite a transformative movement. A single spark of positive change can rapidly escalate into a blazing inferno. The more eloquently and persuasively you advocate for your newly adopted, eco-conscious practices, the more readily others will embrace similar sustainable lifestyles, mirroring your commitment. Lead by example.

Utilize the power of technology. Social media can be a powerful tool for raising awareness about environmental justice issues, mobilizing communities, and holding corporations and governments accountable. Use social media platforms to share information, amplify the voices of marginalized communities, and engage in constructive dialogue with others. Use digital tools to monitor environmental conditions in your community, gathering data that can be used to advocate for policy change. Technological resources are becoming increasingly accessible, and their utilization in the environmental justice fight must be embraced and leveraged effectively - with precision, clarity, integrity, and without bias.

Foster intergenerational dialogue. Environmental justice is not just about protecting the environment for today; it's about ensuring a healthy and sustainable future for generations to come. Engage young people in environmental initiatives, mentoring the next generation of environmental advocates and leaders. Share your knowledge and experiences with them, inspiring them to carry the torch and continue the fight. This intergenerational collaboration is key to building a movement that is sustainable over time.

Embrace continuous learning and adaptation. The challenges of environmental justice are constantly evolving, demanding that we remain adaptable and open to new ideas and approaches. Stay informed about the latest research and technological advancements in the field. Critically evaluate existing strategies and be willing to adjust your approaches as needed. The pursuit of environmental justice requires continuous learning and a willingness to evolve our strategies to meet the dynamic nature of the challenges we face.

The fight for environmental justice is a marathon, not a sprint. It demands persistent effort, unwavering commitment, and a willingness to work collaboratively with others. It requires us to step outside our comfort zones, engage in difficult conversations, and challenge the status quo. The stakes are too high otherwise. The future of our planet and the well-being of future generations depend on our collective action, there is no planet B, only Earth. It is your action, your engagement, and your unwavering commitment that will ultimately determine the legacy we leave behind – a legacy of environmental justice and a truly sustainable world for all. Let us rise to the challenge and ensure that the fight for a healthier planet and a more equitable future continues with renewed vigor and unwavering determination no matter the circumstances, for our earth, for every living being on this planet, and for future generations yet to be born.

www.ingramcontent.com/pod-product-compliance
Lightning Source LLC
Chambersburg PA
CBHW051210120626
46547CB00013B/1290